5/2019

The Nameless and The Faceless of the Civil War

A Collection of Poems & Essays

LISA G. SAMIA

DESTINY WHISPERS PUBLISHING, LLC
TUCSON, ARIZONA
WWW.DESTINYNOVELS.COM

Copyright © 2018 by Destiny Whispers Publishing, LLC

"THE NAMELESS & THE FACELESS OF THE CIVIL WAR"
LISA G. SAMIA, Author
Destiny Whispers Publishing, LLC
ISBN-13 # 978-1-943504-31-2
ISBN-10 # 1-943504-31-8

ALL RIGHTS ARE LEGAL PROPERTY OF THE AUTHOR AND PUBLISHER

Editing, Graphic Art Design, & Formatting:
Leslie D. Stuart, Creative Director / Executive Editor
www.DestinyNovels.com and www.DestinyRose-Reads.com

Some photographs within this collection were taken on location by the author, Lisa G. Samia, and cannot be used or reprinted without written permission. www.LisaSamia.com

The back and front cover are the author's own photos taken April 2017 at Manassas National Battlefield Park, Manassas, Virginia.
Back cover photo: "The Stone Bridge"

"Bundle of Twigs" illustrations used to symbolize the hardships of the Civil War were created by Shannon A. Reedy; exclusive use, all rights reserved.

"Unknown Confederate Soldier" sketch created by Shannon A. Reedy.
All original artwork is property of the artist, exclusive permission given for Destiny Whispers Publishing, LLC, all rights reserved.

Destiny Whispers Publishing, LLC
3015 W. Sky Ranch Trail
Tucson, AZ 85742

www.DestinyNovels.com
www.LisaSamia.com

Introduction

From the Author, Lisa G. Samia

"The Nameless and the Faceless of the Civil War" is a collection of 28 poems and 28 essays along with a selection of corresponding photos, sketches, and historical quotes.

The inspiration of the collection comes from the very first poem and essay on Michael Dougherty of the 13th Pennsylvania Calvary. Michael was captured and imprisoned in several Confederate prisons such as Pemberton, Barrett's, Libby, Belle Island and finally served the duration of his sentence at Andersonville Prison in Andersonville, Georgia.

Over the course of the 23 months and 17 days he was confined to prison, Michael kept a diary. It was only after I read the diary, especially regarding his confinement at Andersonville that the horror of this death camp came to life.

Overcrowding, starvation, madness and sickness were prevalent throughout the prison. And it was Michael's daily written count of men who were dead or dying, stating them as numbers without names or faces, that the inspiration for this collection was brought forth.

What of all of those thousands of soldiers, who were they? History tells us that after the Civil War many of these soldiers were eventually identified, yet what became of the ones who were not? And what about the civilians of the Civil War, those who starved to death, fell to disease or simply died of a broken heart? What became of them?

Most of the poems and essays in this collection are based upon actual historical facts about a person or an event of the war. The narrator in each poem is an imagined civilian or soldier who was lost to history, yet through this creative venue is telling their story of what is was like to be at Shiloh, or be tended to by Louisa May Alcott, or watch John Wilkes Booth die on the front porch of the Garrett farm on April 26, 1865.

The corresponding essays are the factual representation as provided by history, along with my thoughts and feelings.

The result of the combination of the narration with rhyme of the poem and the historical reference of the essay brings forth these voices and gives those lost and forgotten souls a chance to be heard, to tell their story and live again.

Professional Literary Review from Eric Swanson, Librettist for *EDWIN*, *The Story of Edwin Booth*, and co-author of the New York Times bestseller, *The Joy of Living*.

In "*The Nameless & The Faceless of the Civil War*," Lisa Samia deftly weaves poetry and essays into a deeply moving portrait of lives lived and lost during the most violent eruption of the conflict that has defined the United States since its foundation, and continues to rage in our time. A truly touching, thoughtful, and insightful work."

To my husband, Jim

The Statue of Michael Dougherty of the 13th Pennsylvania Cavalry.
His prison diary was the inspiration for
"The Nameless and the Faceless of the Civil War."

Andersonville

I ask you God to please hear my prayer
For those of us left crying in despair
Captured prisoners from the North we stay
Left here in prison dying each day
What could we have done, dear Almighty on high
To be tortured each day and left to die
With nea' even enough water to drink
That was not even clean, I am on the brink
Of madness or death whichever comes first
It's Andersonville ... is hell on earth
I see my comrades once so bright and strong
Crumble in pain, this is so wrong
And so each day that God gives me breath
Is another day I beg for death
For surely the Almighty must see
The agony of those surrounding me
In the dark of night we hear the baying hounds
That surrounds the stockade, such haunting sounds
Screeches here and there that pierce the night
That remind us wholly not to fight
For if I could ever escape this evil place
and tell the world of such disgrace
Yet somehow, I hold that history will tell
of the story of Andersonville, the story of hell.

Andersonville Prison

The Prison Diary of Michael Dougherty of the 13th Pennsylvania Cavalry

May 10, 1844 — February 19, 1930

There are some things in history which stay with you long after you have studied them. For me, it was the diary of the Union prisoner of war, Michael Dougherty, of the 13th Pennsylvania Cavalry.

He was captured on October 12, 1863, and spent time in several Confederate prisons including Pemberton, Barrett's, Libby and Belle Island. During his imprisonment he kept a diary. Eventually, Michael was sent to the horrific confinement at Andersonville Prison in Georgia.

And it was while imprisoned in Andersonville that he wrote the heartbreaking entries into his historic diary that inspired this author. The words written by this soldier reached out to me from so many years ago and compelled me to put this collection together. His thoughts and recorded observations of that time inspired me to give all those thousands of soldiers who suffered and died, in the most egregious conditions a voice to tell their story.

Michael wrote almost daily accounts about the conditions and deaths of the men confined with him while in Andersonville. He was imprisoned there from December 1864 until April 1865 but eventually became too sick to write. His final months in prison are unaccounted for in the diary.

With the South surrendering on April 9, 1865, Michael was released on April 12, 1865. Michael returned home to Bucks

County, Pennsylvania on June 27, 1865. He suffered a total of 23 months and 17 days in Southern prisons.

He was awarded the Medal of Honor issued on January 23, 1897, for most distinguished gallantry in action at Jefferson, Virginia on October 12, 1863. Michael passed away in February 1930 at the age of 86.

We hear from Michael Dougherty's own words, as he writes (July 1864) 19th:

"Upwards of seven thousand prisoners have died in the stockade since I came here, not including the number who have died in the hospital." From July 20th: *"One hundred and thirty prisoners died yesterday; it is so hot we almost roasted. There were 127 of my regiment captured the day i was, and of that number eighty-one have since died, and the rest are more dead than alive; exposure and long confinement is doing its work among us."*

Here we have not just an eyewitness to this tragedy, but an unwilling participant of the fact that groups of men were dying daily who had no names and no faces recorded in history. It is for them the *"The Nameless and the Faceless of the Civil War"* was brought forth, being ever mindful those nameless and faceless men were someone's son, husband, father, brother or uncle.

The narrator in most of the collection is recounting a historical scene of the Civil War. I expanded the concept by adding in my imagined personal reflections of the suffering felt by soldiers, civilians, hospital workers, political figures, and all who experienced the vast pain and misery of Civil War.

In the case of Andersonville prison, over thirteen thousand Union soldiers died and were interred in mass graves, unknown and forgotten.

Of course, some were eventually identified. But for those who were never identified and who suffered so long ago, this collection reaches into the past and gives them a voice. A place to tell their tales of compassion, life, death, agony and grief as a reminder to the world that they did not die in vain.

Walt Whitman, taken in Brooklyn around 1870 by well-known photographer G. Frank Pearsall. This author, poet and writer also served as a nurse during the Civil War. — historical archive credit: Ohio Wesleyan University, Bayley Collection.

Walt Whitman

I awoke from a slumber so incomplete
To see the poet Walt Whitman nearest my feet
With the kindest eyes I have ever seen
Full of compassion and a thoughtful gleam
And I asked him to please sit a spell
To send a letter to my mother, a true southern belle
For his kindness extends to both North and South
Of this I am sure, I have no doubt
And as he asks me what shall he write
From the wounded son who is in such plight
And asks me then about my life
Before the war and all this strife
I said to the poet, "I am from a farm"
That was small and obscure and held no harm
A town called Falls Church of such a sight
The prettiest in Virginia, I know is right
And although the doctor says I may survive
It's with no arms now I must try to thrive
And be grateful then I can breathe the air
For so many comrades are left to prayer
And as I told the kind poet of my heart
He said to me before he did part
"Do not fear young man as you go home
Those who love you will never roam
And leave you tender without love
It is the command, from God above."

Walt Whitman

Civil War Nurse
May 31, 1819 — March 26, 1892

Walt Whitman, the second son in a family of nine children, was born on May 31, 1819, to a housebuilder Walter Whitman and Louisa Van Velsor. The family lived in Brooklyn and Long Island in the 1820s and 1830s.

Beginning at the young age of twelve, Whitman began to learn the printer's trade. There he found his passion for the written word. He was a self-taught man who studied and read voraciously, becoming well acquainted with the great works such as Homer, Dante, Shakespeare, and of course, the Bible.

Following his love for words, he worked as a printer in New York City until a devastating fire that ravaged the printing district demolished the industry.

In 1836, at the age of seventeen, Walter Whitman began his career as a teacher, working with students in the one-room school houses of Long Island. He continued to teach until 1841 when he turned to journalism as a full-time career.

Whitman founded a weekly newspaper, *Long-Islander*, and later edited a number of Brooklyn and New York papers. In 1848, he left the *Brooklyn Daily Eagle* on another adventure to become the editor of the *New Orleans Crescent*.

It was in New Orleans that he experienced firsthand the viciousness of slavery, seeing it daily in the slave markets of that city. On his return to Brooklyn in the fall of 1848, he founded a "free soil" newspaper called, *The Brooklyn Freeman* and continued to develop his unique style of poetry.

In 1855, Whitman obtained a copyright on the famous first edition of his collection of poems, *Leaves of Grass*, consisting of only twelve untitled poems and a preface.

This collection grew over the years of his life to include more than three hundred poems, commonly referred to as *"The Deathbed Edition."* His work became an American Classic in literature. He wrote his famous poem *"O Captain! My Captain!"* after the death of Abraham Lincoln in 1865. It is long since understood that it is a mourning poem written in honor of the fallen President.

When the Civil War began Whitman worked as a freelance journalist and visited the wounded at New York City area hospitals. In December of 1862 he traveled to Washington, DC to care for his brother who had been wounded in the war, then decided to stay and work in the hospitals. He lived in the city for eleven years.

This author, poet, journalist and Civil War nurse was overcome by the suffering he saw, so much so, he offered himself to aid the sick, injured, and the dying soldiers.

Once again, history tells us of Walt Whitman's deep compassion for the soldiers he tried to help. The narrator recounts his story of waking up in a hospital to see the poet near him. The words of one soldier lost in history and lost in time is only one of the men who perhaps was tended by Walt Whitman. His words reach past the lines of North and South to tell his story of the compassion shared by the Civil War nurse.

An ambulance drill at the Army of Potomac Headquarters
near Brandy Station, Va., March 1864.
— Library of Congress

Field Hospitals outside Washington, D.C.
— Civil War Trust

Wounded

I shall never forget as long as I have life
The lament of the wounded that Fredericksburg night
Of the freezing cold and the desperately hurt
The cries unlike anything on earth
Some I heard whispering to those at home
As if they were there to comfort and had known
And whispered back that all will be fine
"Come home now, it is your time"
But home is not the place of hearth and love
But rather to God our Savior and Divine above
And like winged Seraphs of heaven who reign supreme
Proclaiming to all that our Christ is King
So too shall all of those who suffered that night
Be brought to sit with our God, immortal in might

The Casualties of the Civil War

Historically the Civil War was America's bloodiest war. The violence of the battles such as Gettysburg, Fredericksburg, and Shiloh was shocking to soldiers and civilians alike. It is estimated approximately 620,000 soldiers died during this violent and bloody war.

Approximately one in four soldiers who fought in the Civil war never made it home. When the war began, neither side had measures and logistics in place to deal with the injured, sick and dying. At that time no National Cemeteries existed to house and honor the fallen. It was also estimated one in three Southern homes lost at least one family member during the war.

All this loss, all this devastation. It brings to the forefront questions regarding what truly became of the wounded soldiers on the battlefront. Did they rejoin their unit? Did they return home or did they die?

Added to this devastation is the knowledge that one in thirteen men did survive the war, but returned home with limbs missing, making it impossible for those who worked as laborers or on farms to earn a living. Due to this fact tens of thousands of families slipped into privation and destitution.

We hear the voice of a wounded soldier, with neither North or South declared in this poem. Just a soldier who is one of the souls lost to history, who suffered and died as a result of his wound and telling us of his pain. We add this lost voice to the 620,000 who died in America's bloody Civil War.

"We are scattered, stunned; the remnant of heart left alive is filled with brotherly hate... Whose fault? Everybody blamed somebody else. Only the dead heroes left stiff and stark on the battlefield escape."

— Mary Boykin Chesnut, Civil War Diarist

"... poor boy! I never knew you,
Yet I think I could not refuse this moment
to die for you, if that would save you."

— Walt Whitman

Dead soldiers in front of Dunker Church.
Historic photo of Antietam Battlefield from the Library of Congress

Official photograph of the dead along the Hagerstown Pike.
– Library of Congress

Antietam

It was an early fall day so full of delight
When we heard it was soon time to fight
Upon the rolling swells of the beautiful glen
The Maryland countryside, it was called then
A place named by a creek
Antietam, it is we seek
And so I thought how this place could be
The center of such a site that would see
The most horror and death known to date
Our Southern boys, all sent to their fate
Our General Lee whom we love
Followed him like Divine from above
And marched strong by a sunken road
"Hold your ground" is what we were told
And as those Yankees made their advance
The sunken road became our defense
And so how many from both sides died this day
Lined up in piles as I began to pray
And wondered how it was that I should be alive
When so many that day did not survive

The Battle of Antietam

September 17, 1862
Sharpsburg, Maryland

The Battle of Antietam also known as the Battle of Sharpsburg, particularly in the Southern United States, was fought on September 17, 1862 between Confederate General Robert E. Lee's Army of Northern Virginia and Union General George B. McClellan's Army of the Potomac. The fighting occurred near Sharpsburg, Maryland and along Antietam Creek as part of the Maryland Campaign.

Antietam was the first field army–level engagement in the Eastern Theater of the American Civil War to take place on Union soil and is the bloodiest single-day battle in American history with a combined total of 22,717 soldiers who died were wounded, or went missing.

McClellan had halted Lee's invasion of Maryland, but Lee was able to withdraw his Army back into Virginia without interference from the cautious McClellan.

The General's refusal to pursue Lee's Army led to his removal from command by President Abraham Lincoln in November of that year.

Although the battle was tactically inconclusive for either side, the Confederate troops were the first to withdraw from the battlefield, making it a strategic Union victory. It was noted as a sufficiently significant victory which gave Lincoln the confidence to announce his Emancipation Proclamation and discouraged the British and French governments from pursuing any potential plans to recognize the Confederacy.

As we read and understand the historical details of the Battle of Antietam, more than just facts and strategic maneuvering become clear. We become aware of the horror for this event to earn the distinction of being the bloodiest single-day battle in American history.

Think for a moment of that statement, the bloodiest single-day battle in American History and the combined 22,717 dead, wounded or missing soldiers who fought on that terrible day in September 1862. How many of them were never identified? Again, more numbers added, some without names or faces.

The tenor of the poem is one of disbelief coming from a Confederate soldier who cannot believe he survived the carnage of that bloody and most grievous day. Perhaps he is also thinking of the many dead comrades that littered the Maryland countryside, the many who were lost as nameless to history, yet brought forth here by a Confederate soldier's voice telling of his experience of the Battle of Antietam.

Original sketch, "Unknown Confederate Soldier," of the headstones amassed at the Springwood Cemetery in Greenville, South Carolina.

Created exclusively for this collection by artist, Shannon A. Reedy.

Nameless & Faceless

I stood amongst the hundreds of stones
That lined the graveyard filled with bones
And wondered of those that said "Unknown"
Gone to glory and upon a throne
Of heavenly laurels in the clouds above
I wonder then, who did you love?
Were you married with a child or two
Who did they look like eyes of blue?
But with no name or face for me to see
The soldier who lies unknown, God help him please
For no one should die without a trace
Without a name given, not even a face
So as I stand amongst the hundreds of stones
You did not die in vain "Unknown"
For I am here and here I shall stay
To be kindred to all and forever to pray.

The "Unknown's" of Battle

When one sees gravestones with the word "Unknown" chiseled into the cold gray stone that are prevalent in many of our Civil War burial grounds, a sense of wonder and sadness about those who are buried there permeate our thoughts.

This author has walked through several Civil War battlefields and cemeteries in Gettysburg, Manassas, Fredericksburg, and Stone's River and with each visit there are some headstones with only the name of the State and the number of casualties.

Once again, with no name and no face.

It is with this in mind we wonder as to who they were, someone's husband, father, uncle, brother, and son. And wonder still as to those left behind in homes far away from their loved one's anonymous death.

It is this very thought, as well as the inspiration from the Prison Diary of Michael Dougherty to honor those gone too soon from us and in the most egregious and selfless manner, that these "unknown's" shall not have died in vain.

But here in this collection, again, are the voices of those who were taken so violently, in valor and in bravery, soldier and civilian are not forgotten by this author and never will be.

"It is well that war is so terrible,
or we would grow too fond of it."

— General Robert E. Lee

"My plans are perfect, and when I start to carry
them out, may God have mercy on Bobby Lee,
for I shall have none."

— Major General Joseph Hooker
"Fighting Joe"

Louisa May Alcott, famous author and civil war nurse.
Her book "Hospital Sketches" is a collection of four letters
penned home to her family living in Concord, Massachusetts
about her experiences during the Civil War.

Miss Louisa

As I rested and took a look to see
Miss Louisa May Alcott tending me
This hospital in Georgetown of where I now sit
To where our wounded come and admit
That we may not be long for this time and place
The doctors, the doctors cannot keep pace
With the many of those with fever and chill
Oh yes indeed, those too can kill
And the many with wounds that cannot be right
Are left to Heaven and the Almighty's might
For my wound so deep, which I cannot see
Somewhere in my lung, it seems to be
But I have heard this cannot be cured
And a slow suffering death is assured
But it was Miss Louisa who came to understand
That I will be seeing heaven, this was not planned
And so she sits with me as I slip from this earth
Her kindness is beyond all I am worth
She holds my hand as I say goodbye
To the kind Miss Louisa, I fear I shall cry

Louisa May Alcott

November 29, 1832 — March 6, 1888
Civil War Nurse

It is a fact of history that Louisa May Alcott, the author of *"Little Women,"* worked as a Civil War nurse for about six weeks in late 1862, serving at the Union hospital in Georgetown, outside of Washington DC.

This information is found in a book penned by Ms. Alcott called *"Hospital Sketches"* published in May 1863. These sketches are actually four letters written to Louisa's father while she worked at the Georgetown Hospital. They are a collection of the author's feelings and observations while serving as a duty nurse.

While the sketches detailed her journey to Washington DC and the dismal appearance of our Nation's Capital during the war, there were several descriptions of some of the patients that she nursed. I believe this one sketch was the centerpiece of her letters.

Louisa describes her interaction with a vital and handsome Virginia man named John, with bonny brown hair and eyes like a child. She quickly realized her initial observation that his wound was not life-threateneing was wrong. This prognosis was quickly dispelled by the hospital surgeon who regretfully informed he would die a slow and painful death.

It is this author's understanding that his injury to the lung was fatal. Louisa was incredulous that such a vital man should die. Resolving herself to that sobering fact, she sat and nursed John for three days until he passed.

As she was holding onto John's hand for such a long time after his death, she wrote:

"It was unsafe for the dead and living flesh to lie so long together but though my hand was strangely cold and stiff, and four white marks remained across its back, even when warmth and color had returned elsewhere, I could not but be glad that, through its touch, the presence of human sympathy, perhaps, had lightened that hard hour."

The image of such a scene touches our imaginations. Perhaps it is John the Virginia blacksmith who is speaking in this poem, reaching out to remind us of the brave and sad death of this soldier of history and his kind nurse, Louisa May Alcott.

Gen. William T. Sherman inspects battlements in Atlanta
Photo by George N. Bernard – Library of Congress

Atlanta, Georgia following Sherman's "March to the Sea" by
by George Barnard on September 1, 1864. – Library of Congress

Atlanta

Stop! Stop! Stop! The barrage of fire
That has besieged Atlanta that is so dire
General Sherman is ever so near
Ripping apart all we hold dear
His march to my City has caused such grief
Hidden behind tears with little relief
Oh, what I see when I focus my sight
Rubble and ruin the most miserable in blight
Where once stood a City so proud
Is hidden now like a shroud
And the mourning cries are heard at every turn
So many gone, yet continue to yearn
And what will happen then
When Sherman comes through with his men
Of what is left of our Rebel ways
God help us through this sad, sad day
To live yet another day and see
The death of Atlanta, no God please

General Sherman's March through Atlanta

November 12, 1864

On this day in 1864, the Union General William T. Sherman orders the business district of Atlanta, Georgia to be destroyed before he embarks on his famous March to the Sea.

When Sherman captured Atlanta in early September 1864, he knew that he could not remain there for long. His tenuous supply line in Tennessee ran from Nashville through Chattanooga, then continued one hundred miles through mountainous northern Georgia.

This Army had just defeated the Army of Tennessee. It was still in the area and its leader, John Bell Hood, swung his men around Atlanta to try to damage Sherman's lifeline. Of even greater concern to Hood was the Confederate Cavalry of General Nathan Bedford Forrest, who was a brilliant commander capable of striking quickly against the railroads and river transports, on which Sherman relied.

During the fall of the city, Sherman conceived a plan to split his enormous army. He sent part of it, commanded by General George Thomas, back toward Nashville to deal with Hood and the Army of Tennessee while the General prepared to take the rest of the troops across Georgia.

Through October, Sherman built up a massive cache of supplies in Atlanta. He then ordered a ruthless and systematic destruction of the city designed to prevent the Confederates from recovering anything once the Yankees had abandoned it.

By one historical estimate, nearly 40 percent of the city was ruined. Sherman would apply the same policy of destruction to the rest of Georgia as he marched onward to Savannah.

Before leaving Georgia on November 15, Sherman's forces had burned the industrial district of Atlanta and left little behind but a smoking shell.

The information above is the historical version of the events leading up to the destruction of Atlanta and the Rebel army. While we can read about the recorded acumen of Sherman's march to the sea, the human element of the destruction of the City of Atlanta is reflected in this poem. Once again, it is a forgotten voice, one heard perhaps for the first time.

We feel the suffering in the voice describing the destruction of the City, feel the anguish the death and privation caused by Sherman's march through Atlanta as he left complete devastation in his wake.

In reading this unknown person's words we can imagine it is from someone whose pain perhaps still resonates today, coming forward to tell their tale of complete and utter destruction of a life lost forever, yet not forgotten.

Shirley's House, also known as the White House, during the siege of Vicksburg, 1863. This house was owned by James and Adeline Shirley and is the only wartime structure remaining inside Vicksburg National Military Park. – Library of Congress

The Letter

It was the summer of eighteen sixty-three
The time of which will never leave me
For on this mid-summer night
I would remember forever in plight
As I read the letter each time and cried
The words written were mistaken, it was a lie
Of a battle called Vicksburg across whose field
Ran streams of blood that did not yield
It was a Minié ball that took your life
Struck you down in the midst of fight
How you must have suffered, my dear dear love
And wondered then about heaven above
It is the words of your General Grant, I read now
Telling me of such bravery you did bestow
Upon the field and through the fight
Leading your men with all your might
And of such valor I did see
The man who now has left me
Dearest Henry, how I wished to see your face
One last time resplendent in grace
Not to think of your sweet suffering soul
Gone now to God to have and to hold.

Siege of Vicksburg

May 18 — July 4, 1863

From the spring of 1862 until July of 1863 Union forces waged an ongoing military campaign that aimed to take possession of the Confederate stronghold located in Vicksburg, Mississippi. The stronghold lay on the east bank of the Mississippi River, halfway between Memphis to the north and New Orleans to the south, a key position.

The capture of Vicksburg divided the Confederate forces and proved the military genius of Union General Ulysses S. Grant. Vicksburg was one of the Union's most successful campaigns of the war. Although General Grant's first attempt to take the city failed in the winter of 1862-63, he renewed his efforts in the spring.

After defeating a Confederate force near Jackson, Grant turned back toward Vicksburg. On May 16, he defeated a force under General John C. Pemberton at Champion Hill. Pemberton retreated back to Vicksburg, and Grant sealed the city by the end of May. In just three weeks' time Grant's men had marched 180 miles, won five battles and captured some 6,000 prisoners.

Many residents moved into tunnels dug from the hillsides to escape the constant bombardments. General Pemberton surrendered on July 4, and President Abraham Lincoln wrote that the Mississippi River "*again goes unvexed to the sea.*"

The town of Vicksburg would not celebrate the Fourth of July for eighty-one years.

In this poem we take a glimpse into the heart of another unknown of the Civil War as we hear the words of a Union soldier's wife reading a letter written to her by General Ulysses S. Grant indicating the loss of her husband.

Again, this letter is representative of thousands of letters sent during the Civil War to families, delivering the grievous news of a soldier's death.

While we read the imagined thoughts of a Union soldier's wife, this scene was most assuredly occurring in many Confederate homes as well. For in suffering and death the lines of North and South are most assuredly blurred, the agony of loss shared by all.

The Peach Orchard at Gettysburg, Pennsylvania
Reenactment Scene, June 30, 2013. Author's own photo.

Wait for Me

Is it your face my sweet dear wife
That I see in the depths of night
And haunts and taunts me of a life before
Of laughter and love that begged for more
Wait for me my dear sweet wife
Past the embers of battle that take such life
That hold me frozen in a place and time
When we were young and you were mine
Wait for me my dear sweet wife
I am coming home soon
Of one last battle that shall forever loom
As the end of the war for both South and North
Gettysburg it's called… so we go forth

Battle of Gettysburg

July 1 — 3, 1863

The Battle of Gettysburg, fought from July 1 to July 3, 1863, is considered the most important military engagement of the American Civil War. After a great victory over the Union forces at Chancellorsville in late June of 1863, General Robert E. Lee marched his Army of Northern Virginia into Pennsylvania.

On July 1, the advancing Confederates, commanded by General George G. Meade, clashed with the Union's Army of the Potomac at the crossroads town of Gettysburg.

The next day saw even heavier fighting as the Confederates attacked the Federals on both left and right sides of the battlefield. On July 3, General Lee ordered an attack by fewer than 15,000 troops on the enemy's center at Cemetery Ridge.

The assault, known as "Pickett's Charge," managed to pierce the Union lines but eventually failed, at the cost of thousands of rebel casualties. Lee was forced to withdraw his battered army and proceed toward Virginia on July 4.

The result of this historic and bloody battle was that Robert E. Lee never again traveled North to face the Union army. It was said that although Robert E. Lee was a great leader and General, his over-confidence in himself and his Army's infallibility became his greatest mistake in leadership.

Up until Gettysburg the Rebel forces under General Robert E. Lee caused defeat after defeat of the Union armies. The Battle of Gettysburg and the Union victory left the Rebel army depleted of its greatest asset, soldiers.

While it would take until April 9, 1865 for Lee to surrender, the Battle of Gettysburg summoned the beginning of the end of the great Rebel General and his armies.

The narrator here is writing to his wife, and in this poem, we do not know if he was a Union or Confederate soldier. This neutral voice was done in order to show that it mattered not which side he was fighting for, for there were casualties and deaths of over 50,000 men shared by both Armies over the three-day battle. The lines of North and South do not matter for the suffering was shared equally.

This soldier writes he is waiting to be called to battle, only knowing that Gettysburg was the destination and hoping this great battle would end the Civil War. While he hopes for an end to the war, he had no idea that the three-day Battle of Gettysburg would be the single most cause of death and casualties in our American History.

General Robert E. Lee standing in uniform at the Appomattox Court House in Virginia on April 10, 1865 after the South's surrender. The historic photograph was taken by Matthew Brady, 1865.

Ode from a Confederate Soldier

In the quiet stillness of the early April eve
Upon the battlefield, we so believe
Defense of cause for our southern ways
General Lee please come and save
Lead us through the Yankee line
We follow your command though all of time
Yet in this quiet night, our thoughts wander still
To those at home lamenting their fill
Of loves lost or broken beyond repair
Left only to God to lament and despair
And so it came as a flash of light
The end of my life in a Yankee's sight
The Minié ball that crushed my spine
Fired across our Rebel line
The life of me ebbing upon the field in sight
The face of my General compassionate in plight
And as I leave this earth behind
My General's words ever so kind
"Brave with valor so you did fight
Go now to God and follow His light"

Confederate General
Robert E. Lee

January 19, 1807 — October 12, 1870

    Robert E. Lee was born on January 19, 1807 in Stratford Hall, Virginia, as the son of the famous Revolutionary War hero, Henry "Light-Horse Harry" Lee. In following his natural birthright, young Robert Edward Lee seemed destined for military greatness. He graduated second in his class from the United States Military Academy at West Point, class of 1829.

    Two years later, he married Mary Anna Randolph Custis who was a descendant of George Washington's adopted son, John Parke Custis. He served as the superintendent for West Point from 1852 to 1855 and was, therefore, responsible for educating many of the men who later served under him and those who would oppose him on the battlefields of the Civil War.

    In 1855 Lee left the academy, taking a position in the cavalry and in 1859 he was called upon to put down and stop abolitionist John Brown's raid at Harpers Ferry, Virginia.

    Because of his reknowned reputation as one of the finest officers in the United States Army, President Abraham Lincoln offered Lee the command of the Federal forces in April 1861. But Lee declined the position and tendered his resignation from the United States Army when his beloved state of Virginia seceded on April 17, arguing that he could not fight against his own people. Instead, he accepted a general's commission in the newly formed Confederate Army.

    With a masterful victory at Chancellorsville, Virginia in the spring of 1863, Lee had great confidence in his army. The Rebel General was inspired to take the fight North into enemy soil. In late June of 1863, he began a bold invasion of the North, meeting the Union forces at the crossroads town of Gettysburg, Pennsylvania. The Confederate war effort reached its high mark on July 3, 1863 when Lee ordered a massive assault against Union General George Meade's center, spearheaded by Virginians under Maj. Gen. George E. Pickett. The attack known as "Pickett's Charge" was a horrid failure and Lee, recognizing that the battle was lost, ordered his army to retreat.

Taking full responsibility for the defeat, he wrote to Jefferson Davis the President of the Confederacy, offering his resignation, which Davis refused to accept. The Confederates would never again fight that far North.

By the summer of 1864, the Confederates had been forced into waging trench warfare outside of Petersburg, Virginia. Though President Davis named the Virginian General-in-Chief of all Confederate forces in February 1865, only two months later, on April 9, 1865, Lee was forced to surrender his weary and depleted army to Union General Ulysses S. Grant at Appomattox Court House, effectively ending the Civil War.

Lee returned home and eventually became the president of Washington College in Virginia (now known as Washington and Lee University). He remained in this position until his death on October 12, 1870 in Lexington, Virginia.

Although these are all historically factual statements of the Confederate General, in this poem we hear the unknown voice of a soldier under the command of Robert E. Lee. His heartfelt determination to fight for his General is wholly unselfish and courageous. His devotion can be heard through his dying words on the battlefield. Even as he awaits death he is grateful the General has come to his side.

While in our imagination we look at this possible interlude in history, we are left to wonder if General Lee did indeed stop and give comfort to a dying soldier? It is possible, but this "unknown's" voice and story is lost to history. Now it has been given a chance to be heard and live again.

Stone's River National Battlefield in Murfreesboro, Tennessee.
Taken July 2015. Author's own photo

Dearest Joseph

Dearest Joseph, I read your letter today
My heart now aches in the deepest way
For how I miss our life before
The call of duty you did implore
And as you left us that cold December day
To Stone's River, you did say
And by the end of this month it would be told
That a terrible battle would indeed unfold
So tonight I read your letter by light
And picture your sweet face that crossed my night
And wonder still of you so far away
Dearest Joseph, I do pray
Please know that when you are missing me most
You will be guided by the heavenly host
And as the cold wind may sweep your brow
Know it is me bestowing somehow
The love in my heart as I miss your face
Calling your name with such grace
And know that I will forever wait
And not tempt the tides of an unknown fate
But if something should happen, if you should leave
Then hold fast my love, and believe
That I will long for you until such time
That God reunites us and you are mine

Battle of Stones River

December 31, 1862 — January 2, 1863

In late December 1862, the Union and Confederate forces clashed at the Battle of Stones River, near Murfreesboro, Tennessee. On December 31, Confederate General Braxton Bragg's 35,000 troops successfully attacked the 42,000-strong Union force commanded by Major General William Rosecrans. The troops withstood the assault, but retreated to a defensive position, which they held against repeated attacks over the next two days.

On January 2, 1863, another Confederate assault was repelled by overwhelming Union artillery fire, forcing Bragg to order a Southern retreat. With approximately 23,000 total casualties, Stones River was one of the deadliest battles of the war. Rosecrans claimed victory and the battle provided a much-needed boost to Union morale following their defeat at Fredericksburg, Virginia.

The armies collided along Stones River on New Year's Eve. Facing a considerably larger Union force (42,000 Union soldiers to 35,000 Confederates), Bragg launched an attack in bitterly cold morning fog against the Yankees' right flank. The attack was initially successful in driving the Union back, but the Yankees did not break.

A day of heavy fighting brought significant casualties to both sides, their suffering compounded by the frigid weather. The Confederates nearly won but were not quite able to turn the Union flank against Stones River. The new year dawned the next day with each army still in the field ready for another fight.

The strike came on January 2. Confederate General Bragg attacked, going against the advice of his generals and lost the confidence of his Army. The Union troops repelled the assault, and Bragg was forced back to Tullahoma, Tennessee.

The North was in control of central Tennessee, and the Union victory provided a morale boost in the aftermath of the Yankees loss at the Battle of Fredericksburg in December 1862. Stones River was a hard-fought, bloody engagement. The Union suffered approximately 13,000 troops killed, wounded or captured, while the Confederates estimated 10,000 casualties.

President Abraham Lincoln later wrote to Rosecrans:

"...you gave us a hard victory which, had there been a defeat instead, the nation could scarcely have lived over."

The history of the Battle of Stones River from December 31, 1862 through January 2, 1863 at Murfreesboro, Tennessee tells us of the great Generals, both North and South, how Union Major General William S. Rosecrans and Confederate General Braxton Bragg acted out their maneuvers, flanks, positions and strategy.

What it does not tell us, however, are the thoughts and fears of men from both North and South alike who waited on a cold New Year's Eve for the offensive, not knowing what the New Year would bring them. We do know of the massive casualties during the three days and can imagine the untold suffering and loss.

This poem represents the wife of a soldier who is not stated as North or South, for we know the fear of battle and death permeated both the Northern and Southern families alike. There was no distinction for the privation and suffering of those families at home waiting for their loved ones to come back to them.

The narrator here is characteristic of those families. This is a voice lost to history, telling us of the fear of what may happen, and did happen to so many at the Battle of Stones River, over one hundred and fifty-five years ago.

Wounded soldiers gather outside of a field hospital after The Battle of
the Wilderness in May of 1864. — Library of Congress

Amputation being performed at a hospital tent in Gettysburg, PA,
July 1863 — Civil War Photos / National Library of Medicine

Doctor Help Me Please

Oh those words that echo in my heart
Doctor help me as not to part
And help me not to leave behind
My wife, my child so unkind
Yet I cannot save so many I fear
From seeing their maker ever so near
And yet I try and try with all my heart
And still they go, they leave, they part
Today had a young soldier so sweet and pure
What the Minié ball had taken so not to cure
What was left of this young life
Half a body, oh such strife
Yet even with the last of his breath
His hand reached for me in death
And whispered to me "please doctor don't grieve
What is left of me, oh to believe
That heaven above shall be my prize
I see it now in my eyes
And ask of you to please try to save
The one next to me, oh so brave"

Daniel M. Holt, M.D.
1819 — 1868

Surgeon of the Civil War

Civil War doctors did the best they could with the knowledge, medicines, and training available to them. Nothing could have prepared them for the daily horrors of the American Civil War. Physicians were forced to treat wounded patients out of homes, churches, barns or whatever was available to them in the field. It is estimated that doctors treated hundreds of thousands of individual cases during the Civil War.

By far the biggest challenge the doctors faced was disease. Soldiers were more likely to succumb to disease than to suffer death on the battlefield. Of the 620,000 or more of the men who died during the Civil War, roughly 205,000 died from battle wounds while the rest succumbed to illness and disease.

Doctors used the available medicines such as opium, quinine, chloroform and even ordinary whiskey to treat everything from dysentery, diarrhea, smallpox, malaria, typhoid & measles to pneumonia and camp itch.

Perhaps the most gruesome task to be performed by Civil War doctors was amputations. The surgery needed to be quick and their actions decisive in extracting limbs from soldiers who might otherwise succumb to gangrene or infection.

History has in-depth documentation of the life of a Civil War doctor. This poem could be the voice of one of the many soldiers who died from disease or battle wounds. The self-effacing knowledge that this soldier understands death is near and the selflessness of his words to help another is heartbreaking.

Adding to this is the following excerpt from "A Surgeon's Civil War, The Letters & Diary of Daniel M. Holt, M.D.," sharing in his very words the sights and sounds of agony:

"As soon as I opened the door a core of voices cried out, "Oh Doctor! Doctor!! God bless you, doctor Holt, have you come to dress my wounds? Have you brought anything to eat? And a thousand such questions until I fairly broke down, and had to weep like a child. Yet I worked and staggered on until it seemed as if I could not drag one foot before another; and while bending over the bodies of our boys dressing their wounds, my eyes in spite of me, would close, and I have found myself fast asleep over a dying man…"

Perhaps then this was from the benevolent soul of the young soldier, a haunting cry that may have been heard by Doctor Holt a thousand times during his duty as a Civil War Surgeon. *"Doctor, help me please,"* words that remind us not only of the suffering soldiers, but of the surgeons who worked tirelessly to save them.

Major Sullivan A. Ballou
(March 28, 1829 — July 29, 1861)
Library of Congress

My Darling Virginia

The soft spring breeze that touched my face
Reminiscent my darling of your sweet embrace
Of times that I remember oh so well
Your heart your love and our sad farewell
Just know the cause for which we so valiantly fight
Left here in battle in the long long night
As we hear the cries of those
Whose suffering it seems is yet untold
With no comfort that I can share
Left only to God to lament and despair
I rest weary with no sleep
The Yankees so close as to weep
To know that my breath now may be my last
As the attack looms close, hard and fast
Just know then darling Virginia
If I do not live
That I will still be with you as I beg those to forgive
And caress your face with my ghostly breath
What could not be taken from me...not even in death

My Darling Virginia
A Love Letter

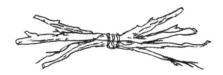

The inspiration for this poem came from one of the most poignant letters ever written in the Civil War. It came from Union Major Sullivan Ballou of Rhode Island to his wife Sarah on July 14, 1861 while in Camp Clark, Washington, DC.

He wrote the letter in advance of being mortally wounded at the First Battle of Bull Run on July 21, 1861 (the first battle of Manassas) and subsequently died from his wounds on July 29, 1861.

The eloquence of Sullivan's writing is as beautiful as it is haunting. In the poem "My Darling Virginia" the unknown soldier is writing to his wife Virginia from the battlefield, not knowing if he would survive or ever see his beloved again.

This poem reflects the thousands of letters like this scripted from a soldier with the fear of death from the battlefield looming over them, men agonizing as each word is written, not knowing if it was to be the last.

The following is an excerpt from the last letter Major Sullivan Ballou wrote to his wife Sarah on the eve of the First Battle of Bull Run, in July of 1861. It is included in this collection as an example of the most heart-rending letter penned during the Civil War:

Headquarters, Camp Clark
Washington, D.C., July 14, 1861

My Very Dear Wife:

"Indications are very strong that we shall move in a few days, perhaps to-morrow. Lest I should not be able to write you again, I feel impelled to write a few lines, that may fall under your eye when I shall be no more."

"But, O Sarah, if the dead can come back to this earth, and flit unseen around those they loved, I shall always be near you in the garish day, and the darkest night amidst your happiest scenes and gloomiest hours always, always, and, if the soft breeze fans your cheek, it shall be my breath; or the cool air cools your throbbing temples, it shall be my spirit passing by.

Sarah, do not mourn me dear; think I am gone, and wait for me, for we shall meet again."

The place where General Thomas J. "Stonewall" Jackson died on May 10, 1863 at Guinea Station, Virginia. Author's own photo

"Let us cross over the river, and
rest under the shade of the trees."

— the final words of
General Thomas J. "Stonewall" Jackson

Stonewall

It was by the campfire that glowed so well
That General Stonewall, best I could tell
Did walk by me and did wholly seem
Confident and determined by any means
And so I did check the date to see
April thirtieth of eighteen sixty-three
Chancellorsville is the name of the town
Over past the Rapidan, it was found
The battle corps of both North and South
Oh, such a battle to bring forth
And in the days that followed the dredge
Of death and despair that led
Of a campaign that did see
The fall of so many it could not be
That our leader Stonewall, I say
Was mortally wounded in early May
He passed away and left this earth
Thirty-nine years after his birth
For such the greatest General I did fight
And loved you see, with all my might

General Thomas J. "Stonewall" Jackson

January 21, 1824 — May 10, 1863

Confederate General "Stonewall" Jackson was known for his bravery and leadership on the battlefield. This courage was exemplified when Jackson acquired his nickname "Stonewall" on July 21, 1861 at Henry Hill outside Manassas, in the Battle of First Battle of Bull Run (First Battle of Manassas).

There are other notable historical facts about Jackson. He was a devout Christian and believed in the divinity of God and was extremely observant of Sunday.

After the First Battle of Bull Run he wrote to his wife:

"Whilst great credit is due to other parts of our gallant army, God made my brigade more instrumental than any other in repulsing the main attack."

An essential element of Stonewall that must be noted as a part of his history, was his love of his family and especially his devotion to his baby daughter, Julia. Beyond his great leadership, Stonewall Jackson was also a father. Due to the circumstances of the war he was not able to see beloved Julia until she was almost four months old. He first saw his daughter on April 20, 1863 at Guinea Station, Virginia.

He had a small reprieve with his family, but by April 29, 1863 the duty of the war called and General Jackson had to leave his wife Mary Anna and baby daughter once more. He proceeded to Chancellorsville, Virginia where he shouldered leadership of the battles.

Word reached Mary Anna that on May 5, 1863 Jackson had sustained an injury and lost an arm. He remained under medical care. On May 10, 1863 the doctors advised Mary Anna that her beloved husband would not survive the day.

She immediately brought the infant Julia to his side. It is noted he never smiled more sweetly as he exclaimed, *"Little darling! Sweet One!"*

His last words were: *"Let us cross over the river and rest under the shade of the trees."*

The narrator of this poem is lamenting the loss of his beloved battlefield Confederate General. This reminds us of the hundreds of thousands of husbands, fathers, uncles and brothers who were lost during the four bloody years of the Civil War. Amid this tragic history, we are also mindful of the heartbreaking loss of General Jackson's greatest joys, Mary Anna and Julia.

Skulls and the unburied bodies of soldiers left in the tangled thickets
and underbrush of the damaged and burned forests west of
Chancellorsville, Virginia from a previous battle.

This became the site of the
Battle of the Wilderness on May 5, 1864

The Wilderness

The sweet smells of the early May morn
Did little for my spirits, I am so forlorn
We look to General Meade to pull us through
Past the Rapidan we marched through
To this place where the brush is so dense
As how this place could make any sense
Or find its way through the tangled leaves
Where we sit under the deepened heaves
It was on this early May morn
The remains of the bodies now torn
Their bones bleached white by the sun
Remnants of uniforms, not sure where spun
Rebel grey or Union blue
The bones yield nothing, not even the truth
Even their skeletons without the eyes
Stare at us in such surprise
That we would come back to this horrid place
Where before it yielded such disgrace
We hear the cries of those in the haze
Who were caught up in the deadly blaze
That took their lives in the most egregious way
Too injured to move they died in such pain
Those screams shall haunt, I am so sure
For those begging for relief, their hearts so pure
Now we move on to Spotsylvania Court House, I hear
Dead comrades wait for me, I am coming near

The Battle of the Wilderness

May 5, 1864

On May 5, 1864 the forces of Union General Ulysses S. Grant and Confederate General Robert E. Lee clashed in the Wilderness forest in Virginia. The day before General Lee had hoped to meet the Union forces, who plunged into the tangled thickets and underbrush of the forests west of Chancellorsville, Virginia. This move through the dense woods was made in order to mitigate the nearly two-to-one advantage Grant possessed as the campaign opened.

The conflict quickly spread along a two-mile front, as numerous attacks from both sides sent the lines surging back and forth. The fighting was intense and complicated. The combatants rarely saw each other through the thick undergrowth. Whole brigades became lost in the woods, smoke from muskets clouding their ability to see barely a few feet ahead. Muzzle flashes from the lint of their guns set the dry forest underbrush on fire. Hundreds of wounded men died in the inferno.

The battle may have been particularly horrifying for the Union troops, who came across skeletons of Union soldiers killed the year before at the Battle of Chancellorsville, their shallow graves recently opened by spring rains. A grim reminder of what fate lay before them in the Wilderness.

By nightfall, the Union was still in control of the major crossroads at the Wilderness. The next two days wrought more battles without a clear victory for either side. Grant eventually pulled out and moved further south toward Richmond, Virginia. For the next six weeks the two great armies maneuvered around the Confederate capital.

The narrator of this poem is a Union soldier describing the battle of the Wilderness. This soldier is also a witness to the shallow and exposed graves of men who fought the previous year at the Battle of Chancellorsville.

Added to that scene is pure horror as the screams of soldiers who were too wounded to escape the burning underbrush caused by the fighting were burned alive and perished in the fire.

This author walked the Battle of Wilderness trail and there is one section that stays with me still. Early into the walk the trail suddenly becomes singular and the overgrowth of bush and burrs become almost overwhelming. Trees still bear scars from being violently torn apart. The silence is so complete it is only interrupted by the sounds of the breeze moving through the dead limbs. The pain there is palpable.

While it is understood that the Battle of the Wilderness certainly was not the bloodiest event of the Civil War, the haunting long-ago sounds of agony can still be felt today.

Jennie Wade died on July 3, 1863 at the young age of twenty, marking the only civilian killed during the Battle of Gettysburg. She is one of the Civil War's most poignant casualties. Photo by William H. Tipton, albumen print on card mount.
– Library of Congress

Jennie Wade

I cannot believe in early July, eighteen sixty-three
That I was destined to die, it was the last of me
Caught we were in the battle to fight
Of North and South it was a horrid sight
It's Gettysburg where these armies engage
Men kill each other with such rage
So as I stood to bake the bread
For our Union men, it was said
That a bullet did cross through the door
And struck me down I fell to the floor
The life of me gone in a blink of an eye
So fast it was, not even to cry
The white light of God did call to me
Of tender twenty years so you see
I leave this earth, please do not cry
For the only civilian who happened to die
But for the thousands of soldiers whose deaths I feel
Do not mourn me for I will kneel
To the Almighty who has called me home
I shall see you all there, by His eternal throne

The Short Life of Jennie Wade

May 21, 1843 — July 3, 1863

Jennie Wade was born on May 21, 1843 in the town of Gettysburg, Pennsylvania. Jennie's father worked as a tailor and unfortunately, over the term of his life, had several skirmishes with the law, eventually becoming confined to the poorhouse. To make ends meet Jennie and her mother worked as seamstresses.

On July 1, 1863 the Battle of Gettysburg began. Jennie along with her mother and brother sought refuge at her sister Georgia McClennan's residence. Her sister had given birth to a son only five days earlier. Unfortunately, that afternoon, as the Union army retreated into the hills, the Wade family lay directly in the lines of battle. Showing remarkable courage under impossible conditions, Jennie went outside to aid the Union soldiers by distributing water.

The following day the fighting continued with flying bullets shattering windows throughout the residence, but Jennie fearlessly aided the soldiers by handing out freshly baked bread. The morning of July 3, 1863 Jennie and her brother went out to gather firewood. After breakfast, she stood in the kitchen preparing the dough to bake once again, only this time a stray bullet found its way through two sets of doors and lodged in Jennie's back. It killed her instantly.

She was the ONLY civilian killed in the three-day battle of Gettysburg. She was just twenty years old.

Found in the pocket of her dress was the photo of a Union corporal, a young man named Johnson "Jack" Skelly. The school of thought is that he and Jennie were engaged. Adding to this heartbreaking story is the knowledge that Jack had been seriously injured during the Second Battle of Winchester in Virginia. He died on July 12, 1863 from his injuries.

Both Jennie and Jack died without knowing the fate of one another. They are both buried at Evergreen Cemetery in Gettysburg, a short distance apart.

The Battle of Gettysburg was the bloodiest battle of the Civil War, claiming over 23,000 Union and 28,000 Confederate soldiers. However, it is the young, brave and short life of Jennie Wade, the only civilian killed in the Battle of Gettysburg, which seems to be its most poignant casualty.

She represents many of the civilians who may have died of starvation or possibly sustained fatal injuries during the war. Names and casualties of many who are unknown to history, but certainly not forgotten.

The William Manse George Cabin.
The only remaining structure from the Battle of Shiloh.

Shiloh

It was early April in the year eighteen sixty-two
That I marched to Shiloh and knew
That this battle would be a bloody fight
Time to kill some Yankees with all my might
Between the forces of South and North
Please General Johnston bring us forth
And guide us through the Yankee line
Determined, resolved and inherently sublime
Oh, but I do see so very many dead
In Shiloh, where the river runs red
From so much death and loss of those
Wounded, dying and full of woe
I see now General Grant is near
Instilling in his men no fear
But I shall stand resolved you see
But if not for the Minié ball in me
I must have fallen sometime that day
For the dead and dying were all to say
"My God my God please do not forsake
All of us here dying in your wake"
I cannot move my eyes strain in the night
Someone comes toward me, I am in fright
God help me please if a Yankee comes near
I know he will kill me, I am in such fear
And oh! Then I did see
The Yankee coming towards me
I could not believe what happened next
As he took his canteen from his breast
And gave me a cup of water to drink
I was so grateful yet could not think
And as he walked away into the night
He said to me with all his might
"Remember that Shiloh it does mean
A place of peace... if only in a dream"

Shiloh

As defined in Hebrew "place of peace"

The word Shiloh as defined in Hebrew means "place of peace." Yet on the morning of April 6, 1862, this 'place of peace' in Tennessee would witness over the next two days 23,000 casualties of men, those numbers combined with the Confederate army under General Albert Sidney Johnston and Federal troops led by Major General Ulysses S. Grant. Creating the bloodiest battle of American history up until that time. The Confederates were defeated in this battle, thus ending any hopes of blocking the Union advance into northern Mississippi.

The history of the Battle of Shiloh does not take into account the stilled voices of those soldiers on the battle lines from those two blood days in early April 1862. The number of casualties, the military positions and the historical facts of the battle do not pay tribute to the human toll of suffering.

The poem comes from a soldier on the battlefield, injured and perhaps dying. One can imagine the agony and fear of such a man whose name and face is lost in history. But hope is offered from an enemy soldier, in this instance a Yankee soldier, giving a cup of life and reminding the injured Confederate soldier what Shiloh means. Perhaps someday peace will reign once again.

How many countless gestures of peace and hope were extended to the enemy armies throughout the Civil War? And how many of those never made it into the history books? Here the word valor comes to mind, a word becoming a fitting tribute to those remembered here and not forgotten.

You must never so much think as whether
you like it or not, whether it is bearable or not;
you must never think of anything except
the need, and how to meet it.

— Clarissa "Clara" Harlowe Barton
Founder of the American Red Cross
and Civil War Nurse

R. H. HENDERSHOT,

Drummer Boy of the Rappahannock, at Fredericksburg.

Robert Henry Hendershot, 8th Michigan Regiment
The Drummer Boy of the Rappahannock

The Drummer Boy

I have to tell the tale of that December night
When our Drummer boy did fight
Of such youth and care he did provide
For all us Union in our pride
Why on that cold December night
His tender years not in sight
Crossed the Rappahannock in the cold and snow
By holding onto our boat you know
And even under heavy fire
From the Rebels it was so dire
He lost his drum yet did not stop
To fight with his comrades and did not drop
The musket to which he found his hands
A Rebel soldier now under his command
Oh so brave, our young drummer boy
Of the Rappahannock it was a joy
And I think he is of such tender years
With valor and elon that brings to tears
The young life we hope is so gallantly spared
Young Robert, you so beautifully compared
To any and all who wear the Union Blue
Our brave drummer boy so very true

Robert Henry Hendershot

December 11, 1850 — December 26, 1925
The Drummer Boy of the Rappahannock

During the Civil War there were countless stories of the bravery and selflessness of soldiers who fought and died during this tumultuous time in our history. Upwards of 40,000 young boys joined the Union and Confederate ranks. Some of these boys were employed as "gofers" serving in camp as musicians, drummer boys, water carriers, and even seen on the battlefield tending to the wounded.

There is one such historical instance of twelve-year-old Robert Henry Hendershot of the 8th Michigan Regiment who performed bravely and acquired the name *"The Drummer Boy of the Rappahannock"* during the Battle of Fredericksburg, Virginia on December 11, 1862.

During this battle Robert crossed the icy Rappahannock River while hanging onto the side of a boat carrying Union soldiers under heavy Confederate fire. His drum was hit by shrapnel, but he did not stop. He showed incredible bravery by picking up a musket, joining the battle, capturing a Rebel soldier and taking him prisoner.

After Robert's discharge it is known that President Abraham Lincoln asked War Secretary Edwin Stanton to find a job for "the gallant drummer-boy" Robert Henry Henderson. This resulted in a position as a messenger in the United States Treasurer's Office.

Subsequent to this, Lincoln endorsed Treasurer Francis E. Spinner's request for the recommendation of Robert to an appointment to the United States Military Academy at West Point.

Lincoln's thoughts were, *"I know something of this boy, and believe he is brave, manly and worthy."*

It was not until late in the war, in March of 1864, that Congress prohibited the enlistment of anyone under the age of sixteen. This occurred only after word spread of a young Cincinnati boy who was killed in the Battle at Resaca, Georgia, May 14—15, 1864. He was one of so many young boys who were lost to the war and never had the opportunity to become men.

Lincoln was also known to absolve those young boys who were sentenced to execution for desertion, so much so, it is recorded the cuffs of his shirt sleeves became threadbare from writing so many pardons.

Perhaps it was the painful and agonizing memory of his own young son Willie, who died too soon at the age of eleven in February, 1862 of bilious fever while in the White House, that affected his deep empathy for those condemned boys.

Richard Rowland Kirkland, the Angel of Marye's Heights.
Official photo from the monument in Fredericksburg, VA.

The Angel of Marye's Heights

Of such despair this cold night brings
Broken men that barely cling
To the last moments on this earth
Mother of God please find our worth
And bring us through this most horrid of nights
That has left us here in such plight
Fredericksburg for us Yankees, of the North
Have stopped us here cannot go forth
For as I sit behind the broken fence
Oh so little for my defense
Against the Rebels behind the stone wall
That were the cause of our terrible fall
We hear such screams of those dying in the night
Begging for water to end their plight
I have never heard of such agony from a man
From those who chose to take a stand
And such bravery should not die
Without a hand or heart to hold and cry
But wait... what do I see?
A Rebel coming towards me
As I raise my rifle to aim and kill
I see he has no blood to spill
For in his hands I see a miracle of some kind
Water for those dying, oh! I am so blind
That I should witness such a kind sight
Mother of God you have given us might
For the Angel you have sent our way
I am on bended knee, if only to pray

Richard Rowland Kirkland

August 1843 — September 20, 1863
The Angel of Marye's Heights

Richard Rowland Kirkland was born August of 1843 on a farm in Flat Rock Kershaw County, South Carolina. He was the fifth son born into the family of Mary and Richard Kirkland. In 1861 he enlisted in the Confederate Army. He was the first man in his family to join the war (before his older brothers).

Richard saw action while assigned to Company E, 2nd South Carolina Volunteer Infantry, but was later transferred to Company G of the same regiment and promoted to Sergeant.

His war action included the First Battle of Bull Run (First Battle of Manassas), the Battle of Savage's Station, Battle for Maryland Heights and Battle of Antietam. It was at the Battle of Antietam where many of his closest friends from Kershaw County were killed.

Richard's bravery and compassion were exhibited on December 13, 1863 when his unit had formed at the stone wall at the base of Marye's Heights near Fredericksburg, Virginia. In the ensuing fighting, he and his unit had inflicted great casualties and loss of life on the Union attackers. That evening the walking wounded made their way to a field hospital, while those who were too severely injured were forced to remain on the battlefield.

The morning of December 14th revealed that over 8,000 Union soldiers had been shot in front of the stone wall at Marye's Heights. Many of those men remaining on the battlefield were still alive but suffering horribly from their wounds and had no water.

Soldiers, both North and South were forced to listen to the cries of the wounded for hours with neither side daring to venture forth for fear of being shot by the enemy. At some point, Richard supposedly approached Confederate Brigadier General Joseph B. Kershaw also from Kershaw County, South Carolina and informed him of his desire to help the Union wounded.

What happened next is the incredible story of valor and compassion. Richard gathered all the canteens, blankets and warm clothing he could find and then ventured out onto the battlefield going back and forth several times to continue his aid. Both sides North and South watched as Richard performed his compassionate care, but no one fired a shot.

After about an hour and a half it became clear to both sides what Richard was doing. According to General Kershaw cries for water erupted throughout the battlefield from the wounded soldiers. Richard did not stop his task until every soldier (Confederate and Union) had been tended, in some way. His actions on the battlefield, incredible selfless acts of compassion and bravery, remain a legend in Fredericksburg to this very day.

Richard later fought in the Battle of Chancellorsville and the Battle of Gettysburg where he distinguished himself for courage. Afterward, he was promoted to Lieutenant. On September 20, 1863 he and two other men took command of a charge near "Snodgrass Hill" during the Battle of Chickamauga. Realizing they had advanced too far from their unit they attempted to return and Richard was shot. His last words were, *"I'm done for...save yourselves and please tell Pa I died right."*

The narrator of the poem is another unknown to history. But through his eyes and longing of heart, we see and hear the voice of the past, recounting the acts of Richard Rowland Kirkland, an ordinary soldier whose compassion and love for his fellow man was greater than any fear for his own short and brave life.

And it is because of his compassion and bravery that I believe he is not just known as the Angel of Marye's Heights, but more than likely a true angel in heaven.

Example of letters sent home from Civil War soldiers

TENT SCENE.—SOLDIERS WRITING HOME TO THEIR FRIENDS.   SKETCHED BY OUR ARTIST.   See page 218.

From New York Illustrated News, August 5, 1861
New York State Library / NYSED.gov

Dear Mrs. Stevens

Dear Mrs. Stevens as I sit and write
Of how your boy Johnny died last night
Such times of him I remember to say
His love of family by Boston Bay
The cobblestones of his neighborhood streets
Footprints of heaven he said under his feet
Know dear Mrs. Stevens as sit and write
Of such valor of how he did fight
I send to you now a lock of his hair
Pressed curls of ivory how very fair
And remember those eyes like I have never seen
Sublime, resplendent like an ice blue stream
But of such things I mention to you
Heaven is happy and glorious in hue
For as I sat next to him on his very last night
And held his hand with all my might
He said to me then, just before he left
That I should write you on his behest
To tell you of your brave, brave son
Of how he fought for the freedom and won
That place in our hearts forever it will be
For the sweet sweet Johnny, we shall not again see

Dear Mrs. Stevens

A letter from the Battlefield

While this poem does not in fact reflect any specific historical Civil War event, it does represent the thousands of letters sent by fellow soldiers to their fallen or wounded comrade's loved ones at home. They were sharing in some cases, the last moments of a soldier's life.

In this poem, the Union soldier is writing to the mother of his comrade "Johnny" referencing the Back Bay of Boston and the cobblestone streets of his boyhood. This representation could also be repeated to those who fought for the Confederacy for as we know the death and grief of the Civil War was not limited to just one side.

It is an example of the dying declaration from a fatally wounded soldier on the battlefield, and the friend who recounts his last moments to his mother. The friend clips a piece of his dying friend "Johnny's" hair and includes it in the letter.

It is known from history that on occasion the dead soldier's canteen, Bible or other personal items found their way into the packages sent home from the battlefield or hospital.

This is a poignant reminder of the hundreds of thousands of men who died so far away from home. Their very last words to their loved ones often scripted by a fellow soldier or hospital worker. As in the case of the poem, "Dear Mrs. Stevens," it is a tragic reflection of unimaginable loss.

Below is the historic letter written by
President Lincoln on December 23, 1862 to Fanny McCullough.

"In this sad world of ours, sorrow comes to all;
and, to the young, it comes with bitterest agony,
because it takes them unawares."

"Abraham Lincoln Speaks Words that Transformed a Nation"
— The Gilder Lehrman Institute of American History and
The Morgan Library and Museum

President Abraham Lincoln in his last formal portrait sitting on
February 5, 1865 in Washington, DC by Alexander Gardner.
He would be assassinated ten weeks later.

A Deep Latent Sadness

It was on an ordinary day like a dream it seemed
That I stood in Washington and gleamed
Drilling with my corps until I could no longer stand
I glimpsed our President, his hat in hand
Who rode by our corps with a nod of his face
A slight smile curved, so filled with grace
But as I noticed his kindly smile
There was something more than his usual guile
I looked with my eyes and could almost see
His latent stare of agony that looked past me
I do not think I could ever define
That honest look in his eyes, just like mine
By the great masters of sculpt and art
Left to them to properly create and start
The sadness in his eyes as he did his review
Of those of us he never knew
But come the journey to Bull Run to fight
The cause of nation as one might
For perhaps he knows as he stares past mine
That we shall not meet until that time
When the angels will call us to come to home
Bound in death to share the throne

President Abraham Lincoln

February 12, 1809 — April 15, 1865
"That deep latent sadness in the expression"

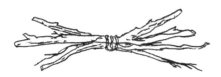

Walt Whitman was a writer and sometimes nurse during the Civil War who brought forth a personal glimpse from his interaction with President Lincoln. Although Whitman was never formally introduced to Lincoln, it was noted he saw him some twenty or thirty times during his Presidency as he rode through Washington DC or to his summer retreat at the Soldier's Home.

His description of their meetings were summed up by Whitman stating, "I see the President almost every day," he wrote in the summer of 1863. "We have got so that we exchange bows, and very cordial ones."

On one memorable occasion, Lincoln gave Whitman a long friendly stare. "He has a face like a Hoosier Michelangelo," Whitman wrote of that day, "so awful ugly it becomes beautiful, with its strange mouth, its deep cut, crisscross lines, and its doughnut complexion."

There was, Whitman wrote, "a deep latent sadness in the expression." He was "very easy, flexible, tolerant, almost slouch, respecting the minor matters," but capable of "indomitable firmness (even obstinacy) on rare occasions, involving great points."

Lincoln was a family man but had an air of complete independence: "He went his own lonely road," Whitman said, "disregarding all the usual ways—refusing the guides, accepting no warnings—just keeping his appointment with himself every time." His "composure was marvelous" in the face of unpopularity and great difficulties during the war.

The somber President had what Whitman saw as a profoundly religious quality. His "mystical foundations" were "mystical, abstract, moral and spiritual," and his "religious nature" was "of the amplest, deepest-rooted, loftiest kind."

Summing Lincoln up, Whitman called him "the greatest, best, most characteristic, artistic, moral personality" in American life.

In reading this poem, and understanding the moving description of the President as provided by Walt Whitman, one can feel what this unknown soldier sees of that ..."deep latent sadness in the expression." It is even more so, as history tells us that President Lincoln gave the full measure of sacrifice to the United States when he was assassinated on April 14, 1865.

Perhaps in some mysterious way that "deep latent sadness in the expression" was actually for himself after having had the premonition he would die while in the White House.

"I remember my mother's prayers
and they have always followed me.
They have clung to me all my life."

— Abraham Lincoln

89

Richmond in ruins, 1865
— Library of Congress

Richmond

My city, my city, what has happened to thee
Lost in rubble and buried in debris
For once stood the capital of the Confederate States
Left in ruin by our hands and own desperate straights
Burned the city as Appomattox rang true
The surrender of the South, so how we knew
That the nation although is as one
Our cause is beaten, forgiveness has begun
And as I stand to gaze at my street
Where once the landed gentry did sleep
And the many nights I stood in awe
Of those sublime, magnificent without a flaw
Left now burned, I see not even a home
Just the bare chimney yet stands alone
Such is Richmond now in ruin and despair
The price paid indeed for such a prayer
As North and South did so horribly fight
So many gone now forever from our sight
All is left what will never come again
Richmond before my sweet sweet glen

The Burning of Richmond, Virginia

The Capital of the Confederacy
April 3, 1865

On Monday morning of April 3, 1865, the ammunition arsenal blew up in the city of Richmond. The massive explosion shattered windows and knocked over headstones at nearby Shockoe Hill Cemetery. Much of the city was on fire, mobs were looting, and chaos ensued.

"Richmond burning," resident Mary Fontaine wrote, *"and nobody to douse the flames."* Rebels soldiers and officers had fled the city, but the fire raged on.

It was the spring of 1865, and after four years of Civil War the Confederacy was dying. The Capital of the Confederacy in Richmond had endured hardships such as food shortages in recent years but had always trusted General Lee to protect them. With the mass exodus of soldiers and officers alike, the proud city had fallen.

The fire was started by the Confederates in advance of the Union march. They set it to destroy anything that the Union may have been able to use.

The fire raged as it destroyed banks, hotels, paper mills, railroad depots, and bridges over the James River. The privation faced by the citizens of Richmond were summed up by resident Nellie Grey:

"We covered our faces and cried aloud." All through the house was the sound of sobbing. It was as the house of mourning the house of death."*

"Was it to this end we had fought and starved...that the wives and children of many a dear gallant friend were husbandless and fatherless? To this end that our homes were in ruins, our state devastated."

Through the annals of history, we can still hear these words of anguish of those Richmond residents who witnessed the destruction of not only the Confederacy, but their city as well.

In this poem, we hear from an "unknown" resident of Richmond who is watching and lamenting the loss and destruction of what was and would never come again. Once again, we are giving a voice to someone lost to history, telling their story of loss, pain, and grief.

A wood engraving from Frank Leslie's Illustrated Newspaper by
illustrator J. Becker showing President Lincoln riding through
Richmond, Virginia on April 4, 1865. — Library of Congress

No More on Bended Knee

Such was the date, April fourth, eighteen sixty-five
The day I knew I was truly alive
For what my eyes beheld that day
The sight of the Emancipator coming my way
It was for him and those who fought
To stop the taskmaster and all who wrought
The scourge of slavery is no more
I see him walking, I must not ignore
And as he made his way through town
Remnants of a City burned to the ground
The ones who are now free follow his gait
Though the City that that held such hate
And so I caught up with all of those
Whose freedom now it was to behold
I watched and listened as they cried out to him
The freedom from the lash, Ah! Such a sin
I walked towards the multitudes gathered around
To hail the Emancipator with a crown
But wait! Then what did I see
Coming through the crowd behind me
An elderly man whose back was bent
From the torturous years of a slave spent
And as he knelt on his knee
Bowing to the one who set him free
I heard the whisper ever so fine
From the man believed so divine
"Kneel to God only," I heard him say
"And thank Him for the Liberty that has come your way."
And with that he held out his hand
To help up the grateful elderly man
The Emancipator looked him square in his face
For they were now equals in this human race
Then he reached for the hand of his little son
I could only think then, we are now as one

Richmond, Virginia

April 4, 1865

On April 4, 1865, President Abraham Lincoln visited the Confederate capital of Richmond. It was only one day after Union forces capture the city. Accompanied by a small group of soldiers and a growing entourage of freed slaves, he walked to the Confederate White House and sat in President Jefferson Davis' chair. He then walked to the Virginia state house and saw the chambers of the Confederate Congress.

Lincoln even visited Libby Prison, where thousands of Union officers were held during the war. The President remained in Richmond for several days in hopes that Confederate General Robert E. Lee's army would surrender, but on April 8 he returned to Washington. The surrender would occur the very next day April 9, 1865 at Appomattox Court House.

In this poem, the narrator is one of the freed black slaves of the South who watches as Lincoln walks through the burned Confederate Capital of Richmond. He follows the band of former slaves and soldiers as he walks through the city. The narrator witnesses a former slave who is an elderly man, as he stops and kneels before Lincoln.

A poignant fact of history is well noted, as the ever-humble Lincoln reminds the elderly man to *"kneel to God only and thank him for the liberty you will hereafter enjoy."* Many watched as their eyes met in the understanding of equality. Then Lincoln took the hand of his youngest son Tad and continued through the city. Tragically, several days later on April 14, 1865, President Lincoln was assassinated as he watched a play at Ford's Theater in Washington, DC.

"America will never be destroyed from the outside.
If we falter and lose our freedoms, it will be
because we destroyed ourselves."

— President Abraham Lincoln

"What a cruel thing is war: to separate and
destroy families and friends, and mar the purest
joys and happiness God has granted us in this
world; to fill our hearts with hatred instead of love
for our neighbors, and to devastate the fair face of
this beautiful world."

— General Robert E. Lee

Appomattox Court House, Virginia

The home of Wilmer McLean where General Robert E. Lee
surrendered to General Ulysses S. Grant on April 9, 1865 ending
the Civil War. It was said by Wilmer McLean that "the war began
in my front yard and ended in my front parlor." The McLean family
left Massasass, Virginia after their home was involved
during the First Battle of Bull Run in 1861.

Appomattox Court House

Today I stand at the house of Wilmer McLean
The meeting place that I did not dream
Would become the end of our cause
The truth of which gives me pause
And as I stand with my comrades in gray
Noble in defeat in every way
We watch as General Lee, so fine and right
Rides upon on Traveller, so grey and white
And watch with silence as we all stare
Tis the last of our General, oh such despair
There comes now such an ache of heart
That I will not see him and have to part
From which I would fight, give my dying breath
And give over my life to a wanting death
So as I stand here in the front yard
A place I know will soon be avowed
As the place the South, it is true
Surrendered itself, I am so blue
I stand tall now watching the sight
No shoes, no food, but with all my might
Words cannot say truly of how deeply I lament
The years of bloodshed that was spent
Only to now see this fateful day
My South in defeat, I can only pray

Wilmer McLean

May 3, 1814 — June 5, 1882

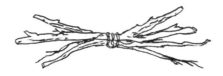

Wilmer McLean was a grocery wholesaler in Manassas, Virginia. His home was involved in action during the First Battle of Bull Run in 1861. Trying to escape the war, Wilmer moved his family to Appomattox Court House in Virginia. This is one of those ironies of history since it was the residence of Wilmer McLean at Appomattox Court House that eventually served as the surrender point of General Robert E. Lee to General Ulysses S. Grant, on April 9, 1865 thereby ending the Civil War.

Later, McLean is noted to have said, *"The war began in my front yard and ended in my front parlor."*

In this poem a Confederate soldier is standing outside the Wilmer McLean House at Appomattox Court House in Virginia. He is witnessing the South admit defeat, and bears witness to the day Confederate General Robert E. Lee surrendered himself to the Union General Ulysses S. Grant on April 9, 1865.

Here he is expressing the loss of the war, the disbandment of the Confederate army and gives the final farewell to his beloved General. While it is also understood the defeat of the Southern forces resulted in the Union welcoming back all those seceded states, in the case of this narrator, the soldier shares a glimpse of what it must have felt like to be there on that day of surrender.

A reminder once again of those voices lost to history and in this collection given the opportunity to have their voices heard and share their story that perhaps was never told.

"The war is over — the rebels are our countrymen again. The war is over, the Rebels are our countrymen again, and the best sign of rejoicing after the victory will be to abstain from all demonstrations in the field."

— From General Ulysses S. Grant upon stopping his men from cheering after Lee's surrender at Appomattox Court House on April 9, 1865

View from Ford's Theater, Washington DC on the night of
April 14, 2015 marking the 150th anniversary of the assassination
of President Abraham Lincoln. Author's own photo.

The Third Floor

Oh, such the sight these eyes did see
On the night of April fourteenth, that brought me to my knee
From the third-floor window I did peer
To witness the scene on the street so near
Such shouts and screaming that pierced the night
Watched as they carried the President in sight
And into the house that I call home
Petersen it is; the name forever known
My blood froze cold ever with the thought
Our President I heard has been shot
For want to know, yet feared to see
The President that helped to free
All those oppressed and wanting souls
Bondage is broken so it is told
I crept down the stairs as silent as could be
To help the man who did not know me
I watch them now from the first floor
Of the profusion of soldiers, please no more
The house therein seemed to burst at the seams
In the midst of panic and fear it did bring
I wound my way to the back of the floor
To see the great man who ended the war
But I was pushed aside and pushed away
Yet in my heart I prayed and prayed
And finally ran to see the man
To try to aid him and hold his hand
I tried and tried, yet could not get close
Please Almighty heavenly host
Yet then in the early start of day
I did hear something that came my way
"He belongs to the ages" it was said
From the little bedroom where he had bled
And as I was once again pushed far away
From the President I loved and could not stay
That I will never forget the man who once met my eyes
Smiled then at me once, and so now I cry

The Petersen House

Where Lincoln Died
Washington, DC — April 14 & 15, 1865

On the night of April 14, 1865 mortally wounded President Lincoln was carried from Ford's Theater to the home of William and Anna Petersen, across the street at 516 10th Street to a back bedroom on the first floor of the house. While the Petersen family assisted as much as they could, their home quickly became crowded with over ninety people who visited that night to pay last respects to the dying President. Soldiers guarded the front door and the roof to secure the growing crowds gathering around the home. Doctors cared for the President, but the wound was fatal. At 7:22 am, April 15, 1865 the great and compassionate President Abraham Lincoln took his last breath.

History rings out with these terrible events and stories from those who were present at the Petersen House that night. In this poem an unknown resident witnesses the events unfold from the third floor, and whose only desire was to find their way to the back bedroom on the first floor. It speaks of that longing as to see the President, but was pushed aside and pushed away, yet kept trying. Finally, the person became close enough to hear War Secretary, Edwin Stanton say, *"Now he belongs to the ages,"* just moments after the President passes away.

This poem is for all who were somehow touched by President Lincoln and whose stories and interaction, however brief, never made it into the history books. As in this case, a passing smile or glance in acknowledgment from Lincoln to this unknown person was enough to provide a voice lost to time, speaking now to share their grief.

"He (Abraham Lincoln) said he wanted to visit
the Holy Land and see those places hallowed by
the footprints of the Saviour. He was saying there
was no city he so much desired to see as Jerusalem.

And with the words half spoken on his tongue,
the bullet of the assassin entered the brain, and the
soul of the great and good President was carried by
the angels to the New Jerusalem above."

— Mary Todd Lincoln

Asia Booth Clarke, the older sister to John Wilkes Booth.
This author, poet, and Booth family chronicler was incredibly close
to John and remained so for all of their lives. The assassination
of President Lincoln by her brother devastated her.

Tudor Hall
Bel Air, Maryland

I remember it well the sweet sweet dreams
Of where I called home, forever ago it seems
Cast now in shadows of what once was
Never to come again gives me such pause
Of a boyhood I can only see
That was sublime, rich and meant to be
The love I have as a mother's son
Left only to God, thy will be done
And whose laughter do I hear in my mind
Sweet kind wonderfully sublime
A dear sweet sister's love
Forever ago, as if from above
And such times in our most early of years
Is gone now and left only to tears
But I remember it all so very well
Tudor Hall it was called, yet I am in hell
For all I have done and most assuredly deceived
The one true cause of which I believed
And leaves me here cast in the swamp and cold
Running from all yes it was so bold
And as I wait for those to help and aid
Left only to despair and prayed
And think then of my boyhood place
And times of joy, now times of disgrace
In Bel Air it was, in the greenest glen
Goodbye sister Asia, never again

Asia Booth Clarke

November 19, 1835 — May 16, 1888

Asia Booth Clarke was the older sister to John Wilkes Booth. History tells us she was born in Bel Air, Maryland and was about two years old before her parents Junius Brutus Booth, a famous actor and tragedian, and Mary Ann Holmes Booth decided on her name.

It was her father Junius who initially thought of "Aisha" after the Prophet Muhammed's favorite and youngest wife, and her middle name as Frigga because she was born on a Friday. They eventually agreed on Asia Frigga Booth.

She was a sensitive young woman, given to "sulks" yet by all accounts was a loving and devoted sibling and daughter. This writer, poet, and Booth family chronicler gave us invaluable descriptions and insights from her book, *"The Unlocked Book, a Memoir of John Wilkes Booth by his sister Asia Booth Clarke."*

She writes of her brother John:

"Once he burst out with joyous exclamation, 'Heaven and Earth! How glorious it is to live! How divine! to breathe this breath of life with a clear mind and healthy lungs! ... "Don't let us be sad," he would say. *"Life is so short-and the world is beautiful. Just to breathe is delicious."*

The two siblings were extraordinarily close, devoted to one another throughout their youth and remained so even after they left the family farm in Bel Air.

In this poem, the narrator is John Wilkes Booth. He is lamenting the loss of his childhood home and the love of family and especially his sister Asia after assassinating President Lincoln. A haunting possibility of what might have been in John's heart as he lay in hiding and in pain from his broken leg in the Maryland and Virginia countryside.

Asia was devastated by John's act and history tells us her grief was inconsolable. She left the United States in 1868 with her husband John Sleeper Clarke and her children, Asia, Edwin, Adrienne, Clarke, Lillian, Wilfred and Joan to reside in the English countryside.

Unfortunately, her life there was not a happy one. Isolated from her family in the United States she died at the age of fifty-two in 1888.

Her last request to her family was to be buried in the United States at Green Mount Cemetery in Baltimore Maryland, where the Booth family had their plot. Specific to her last request, to be interred next to her brother John who is buried there in an unmarked grave.

It was only after this author's visit to Green Mount Cemetery that the poem was written. The palpable sadness experienced along with Asia's haunting last line of her book: *"So runs the world away,"* provided a poignant glimpse into a sister's grief.

*Hamlet, act 3 scene 2

Two of the few known photos of Richard Garrett's farmhouse

Taken later, after the home was abandoned.
— both photos, Library of Congress

My Front Porch

It was in the early hours of the late April morn
That the very being of my life was torn
For what I witnessed in the dark of day
That even now I so fervently pray
That the injured man who came with his friend
Two Confederates, at their very end
They found refuge with my family's aid
To rest and heal by our green green glade
And as I stood on our front porch
And watched our barn burn, it was torched
By the Union soldiers that came to claim
The men inside our barn, oh such shame
I watched in horror as the injured man
Was dragged to our porch and damned
Shot through the neck, I did see
I ran to tend him as best could be
And even in his deepest pain
His handsome face did refrain
Water I gave him and touched his brow
The whitest of skin, I did vow
And such was the face that looked at me
Compelling and handsome that yearned to be
It was then I saw the gleam around his chest
A gold metal that stood out blessed
The Agnus Dei - Lamb of God, it said
I wondered then about this man and begged
And so I heard him cry out into the night
To the one not near him, it was a grievous sight
"Please tell my mother" he said under his breath
"I died for my country" then welcomed death

Richard Garrett's Farm

Port Royal, Virginia — April 26, 1865

In the mid-afternoon of April 24, 1865 John Wilkes Booth, and his fellow conspirator David Herold, arrived at the farm of Richard Garrett located on Locust Hill in Port Royal, Virginia. Around midday, the fugitives had been at Port Conway, Virginia waiting on the banks of the Rappahannock River.

Both Booth and Herold were fugitives due to Booth having assassinated President Abraham Lincoln at Ford's Theater in Washington DC twelve days prior. As one of Booth's conspirators, David Herold met up with Booth the night of the murder, accompanying him on an unplanned stop at the home of Dr. Samuel Mudd in Charles County, Maryland. The purpose of the stop was to set Booth's leg, which was broken during his jump from President Lincoln's box at Ford's Theater after assassinating him with a single shot derringer.

Both Booth and Herold had spent the last twelve days desperately fleeing into Virginia and to points further South, with the aid of various Confederate sympathizers, eventually ending up at Richard Garrett's farm.

As Booth and Herold waited for the ferry to come, three Confederate soldiers rode up, Willie Storke Jett, Mortimer and cousins Bainbridge Ruggles, and Absalom Ruggles Bainbridge. The three Confederates were heading towards Richmond when they met Booth and Herold.

At first, David Herold told them that he and his wounded brother named "Boyd" were also Confederate soldiers and hoped to join them on their journey South. Becoming suspicious as to Herold's seemingly desperate tone, Jett then asked who they really were.

They were shocked that Herold replied back, *"We are the assassinators of the President."* The three men then rode to the Garrett farm, with Booth and Herold sharing horses with Ruggles and Bainbridge, respectively. The Garretts agreed to care for Booth, whom Jett said was a wounded soldier named Boyd.

The rest is well-known. When the Union troops arrived, specifically the Sixteenth New York Cavalry, they kept Jett under guard near the gate of the farm while the rest surrounded the house and barn. Eventually, Herold surrendered as the barn was lit on fire to smoke out both he and Booth. Boston Corbett of the 16th New York Cavalry fired at Booth inside of the burning barn, shooting him in the neck and paralyzing him. Booth was dragged from the barn, placed under a tree and then onto the front porch of the house. He died around dawn on April 26th.

History tells us what happened leading up to and during the events of that fateful day. The poem as written, however, is describing the events of the early morning hours of April 26, 1865 through the eyes, perhaps, of one of Richard Garrett's ten children. Any number of them could have been watching and recounting what it felt like to be standing on the family's front porch where John Wilkes Booth had been taken to die after being shot through the neck. Perhaps it was the youngest Garrett child, Cora Lee Garrett, the one child in particular Booth was close to, so much so he called her his "little blue-eyed pet."

An interesting yet not widely known fact of history was that John Wilkes Booth had an endearing love for children. Upon his arrival with David Herold at the Garrett farm, John Wilkes Booth engaged several of the Garrett children playing with the five youngest all under the age of ten, inasmuch as his broken leg allowed him to do so. But it was to the youngest child, Cora, that he poured out most of his attention.

On the morning of April 26, 1865, the life of this shadowy and complex figure of American history ended. He asked to see his paralyzed hands and was heard to say, *"Useless, Useless,"* and died on the front porch of Richard Garrett's' Farm. It is left to the imagination what it must have been like to watch this scene unfold. And wonder still of the little child Cora Lee Garrett, John Wilkes Booth's "little blue-eyed pet," who watched as he closed his eyes in death right there on her very own front porch.

John Wilkes Booth, the actor and southern sympathizer
who believed by decapitating the government (President Abraham
Lincoln, Vice President Andrew Johnson and Secretary of State
William Seward) the South would rise again.

Johnnie

I saw your face frozen in time
The eyes beholden and deeply sublime
That captured my sight to your face
The one that haunts me, yet filled with grace
Of such evil deeds, I did read
You believed in a cause, so deceived
Yet could not stop the pangs to kill
Anger hatred was your fill
But then wait, oh what do I see?
The man before the hate who was so free
Songs of love that begged for more
If only you knew me, was mine to adore
For if I could creep back into your time
I would in fact beg you to be mine
And take me resplendent for the days to come
On my knees, my darling my love
Such is the face that haunts my nights
Wait for me darling, with all your might

John Wilkes Booth

May 10, 1838 — April 26,1865

John Wilkes Booth was notably the favorite of the Booth household, born on May 10, 1838 in Bel Air, Maryland the ninth of ten children born to Junius Brutus Booth and Mary Ann Holmes Booth. John was an actor like his father, the great Shakespearean tragedian, Junius Brutus Booth and his older brother, Edwin.

It is this author's opinion that one of the more compelling personality traits of John, or "Johnny" as he was known to his family, was his love of children.

As uncle to his sister Asia's children, he would upon visiting them in Philadelphia, remind them to *"Remember me, babies, in your prayers."*

According to Asia Booth Clarke's letter to her longtime friend Jean Anderson, she wrote...

"Philadelphia. March 3rd 1863...John Booth won a suit of baby clothes at a fair out west and made me a present of them. Need I be more explicit and say the gift was very appropriate? John Booth laughs outrageously at me for having babies. He can't realize it, he says, to think that our Asia should be a mother. He lies on the floor and rolls over with them like a child...."

Yet once again the John Wilkes Booth who this author had researched, specifically from his sister on her recollections on their life together in Bel Air and Tudor Hall as written in, *"The Unlocked Book, A Memoir of John Wilkes Booth, by his sister Asia Booth Clarke,"* his capacity for friendship and love not just to his family is a truly compelling aspect of this shadowy figure of American history.

Additionally, Asia wrote…

"As a boy he was beloved by his associates, and as man few could withstand the fascination of his modest, gentle manners. He inherited some of the most prepossessing qualities of his father, and while that father's finely shaped head and beautiful face were reproduced in him, had had the black hair and large hazel eyes of his mother. These were fringed heavily with long up-curling lashes, a noticeable peculiarity as rare as beautiful. He had perfectly shaped hands, and as a little boy he had clumsily marked across the back of one his initials in India ink.
One great charm of his attractiveness was the fact of his being a good listener. This is an accomplishment perhaps, but it perfected only by the help of an unselfish and charitable disposition."

Also noted in the book *"Sketches of Tudor Hall and the Booth Family,"* we look to the author Ella V. Mahony who came to live at Tudor Hall in 1878 with her husband for additional nuances of John's early life. She writes:

"He was the handsome, daring, good hearted boy, always welcome among his friends here - most welcome at all times."

Many descriptions like this throughout his young life echo the same sentiments as Mrs. Mahoney. These descriptions only add to the chasm of disparity between who he was a youth and young man, to the man who eventually assassinated President Lincoln.

We can also look at his relationships with women, and his ability to exude great longing and passion. Nowhere more noted than by his own words in a letter to a sixteen-year-old Boston girl named Isabel Sumner.

In the book *"Right or Wrong, God Judge Me,"* the Writings of John Wilkes Booth," he pours out his heart to her and his longing is heartfelt:

To Isabel Summer
New York City, 14 July 1864

28 East 19th:
July 14th:

Dearest Friend:
   *"······Dearest Isabel, I can not write to you. I want to talk to
you. I have just travelled over 600. miles . It is now 2/12 A. M. I
am tired and sick. Let that, be an excuse for this miserably written
letter. But the style or manner of my letter be what it may. I LOVE
YOU, and I feel that in the fountain of my heart a seat is set to
keep its waters, pure and bright for thee alone. God bless you.
You see (to follow your wishes, NOT MY - OWN) I call myself your
FRIEND only good night {...} JWB"*

The time period of his liaison with Isabel was the summer of
1864. Yet sometime in early 1865 it is known that John Wilkes
was secretly engaged to Lucy Hale, a Senator's daughter from
New Hampshire. Having heard of the assassination of President
Lincoln by her fiancée John Wilkes it was said:

   *...There were rumours that she had gone, heavily veiled,
aboard the USS Montauk in the Washington Navy Yard to view
the body of Booth which lay in one of the cabins, and upon seeing
it, threw herself on him, sobbing...*

John Wilkes Booth was a young man who was dearly loved by
his family, friends, and of course by women. While here it is
noted two of his loves were Isabel Sumner and Lucy Hale, it is to
our imagination that we hear a voice and feel a heart lost, one
forgotten by time.
   One hundred and fifty-three years after his death this
unknown woman is still waiting to lay claim to this elusive and
shadowy man of history. And one hundred and fifty-three years
after his death we still look for answers to explain his one
unexplainable act.

Acknowledgements

To my husband Jim Samia, for your love.

Historian / Author, Terry Alford –
friend and mentor, thank you.

Elisabeth Cannata for your friendship,
advice, and support.

Director Enrica Jang and her staff at the
Edgar Allan Poe House in Baltimore, Maryland.

The Edgar Allan Poe Museum in Richmond, Virginia.

Leslie Stuart of Destiny Whispers Publishing, LLC,
thank you for believing in this work.

Terri Wilson, President of the Avon Historical Society,
Avon, CT for your support, help and friendship.

Eric Swanson, Librettist for EDWIN, The Story of Edwin
Booth and co-author of the New York Times bestseller,
The Joy of Living.

Jane Kosminsky, Artistic/Executive Director of Great
Circle Productions, Inc., and Faculty the Juilliard School.

The Surratt House Museum

The Dr. Samuel A. Mudd House Museum

Special thanks to all my friends and family
for their support and love.

About the Author

Lisa G. Samia is an award-winning poet and author who loves Civil War History. She devoted three years traveling, researching and writing her historical fiction (on John Wilkes Booth) "My Name is John Singer."

She is a graduate from the University of Massachusetts in Boston and a Boston native. She currently resides in Avon, CT with her husband, Jim.

Lisa's award-winning poetry collection, "The Man with the Ice Blue Eyes" is a compelling collection of love poems that debuted number one on Amazon Poetry for Women in July 2016.

Her article, "John Wilkes Booth, the Son, Brother, Uncle and Actor," has appeared in both the Surratt Courier and in the Samuel A. Mudd Newsletter. She is currently writing the sequel to "My Name is John Singer."

www.DestinyNovels.com
www.LisaSamia.com

Accomplishments

❖ Author of "Don't Be Afraid of Fifty," The Twelve Step Process to Turning Fifty. November 2011.

❖ Author of "My Name is John Singer," a Romantic Historical Fiction on John Wilkes Booth. Endorsed by Great Circle Productions Inc New York, NY. Endorsed by New York Times best-selling co-author of "The Joy of Living," Eric Swanson and author of books & lyric's of EDWIN, The Story of Edwin Booth. September 2016

❖ Author of "The Man with the Ice Blue Eyes," Romantic Poetry Collection of love and heartache. Debuted number one on Amazon.com for Women's Poetry, July 13, 2016. Included in collection are two award winning poems from the Connecticut Authors and Publishers Association

❖ Author of "The Nameless and the Faceless of the Civil War." A collection of 28 poems and 28 essays on the historical representations of Civil War events through the narrative of poetry. April 26, 2018

❖ Appearances in April 2017 at Barnes & Noble Bel Air, MD and Fairfax, VA and August 26, 2017 at the Barnes & Noble, Baltimore MD

❖ Appearance at the Hartford Public Library, Hartford, CT March 10, 2018

❖ Appearance at the Barnes & Noble, Fairfax VA – May 5, 2018

❖ Presented program at the Poe House and Museum in Baltimore, MD June 11, 2017 on Annabel Lee

❖ Presenter/speaker at the Poe Museum Richmond VA, May 6, 2018 on Annabel Lee

❖ Interviewed by Avon Life on "The Nameless and the Faceless of the Civil War." March 2018

❖ Interview with the Hartford Courant, April 2018 on "The Nameless and the Faceless of the Civil War."

❖ FINALIST for the 2018 Artist in Residence Program – National Parks Arts Foundation Gettysburg 2018.

❖ Awards from the CT Authors and Publishers Association Writing Contest: 2013-2014, 2nd place Essay and Honorable Mention Poetry; and awarded in 2014-2015: 1st place Poetry.

Member of the following
Historical Societies:

- ❖ Ford's Theater, Washington, DC
- ❖ Lincoln Cottage, Washington, DC
- ❖ The Surratt Society, Clinton, MD
- ❖ The Junius Brutus Booth Society (Tudor Hall), Bel Air, MD
- ❖ The Civil War Trust
- ❖ Dr. Samuel A. Mudd House Museum, Waldorf, MD
- ❖ The Avon Historical Society, Avon, CT

- ❖ Graduate of University of Massachusetts Boston. Originally from Boston MA and currently resides in Avon, CT.

References & Historical Sources

Books

- ❖ "A Surgeon's Civil War, The Letters & Diary of Daniel M. Holt, M.D." by James M. Greiner, Janel L. Coryell, & James R. Smither
- ❖ "The Best Little Stories from the Civil War," by C. Brian Kelly with Ingrid Smyer, Originally published: Charlottesville, Va. — Montpelier Pub., c1994.
- ❖ "Asia Booth Clarke, The Unlocked Book, A Memoir of John Wilkes Booth with a foreword by Eleanor Farjeon" — G.P. Putnam's Sons New York 1938
- ❖ John Wilkes Booth, "Right or Wrong, God Judge Me," The Writings of John Wilkes Booth, Edited by John Rhodehamel and Louise Taper, University of Illinois Press Urbana and Chicago
- ❖ "Sketches of Tudor Hall and the Booth Family" Copyrighted 1925 by Ella V. Mahoney, hardcover
- ❖ "Fortune's Fool: The Life of John Wilkes Booth" by Terry Alford, Oxford University Press 04/14/2015

Articles

- ❖ 'Richmond At Last!': The Final, Fiery Days of the Confederacy http://www.washingtonpost.com/sf/style/2015/03/27/wars-end/?utm_term=.b7831517bd07-The Washington Post -Michael E. Ruane March 27, 2015
- ❖ Stonewall's Greatest Joy, by Chris Mackowski — Civil War Times August 2017

Quotes

- ❖ Mary Todd Lincoln Quote: He (Abraham Lincoln) Said He .., http://www.azquotes.com/quote/1404984Abraham Lincoln Quotes
- ❖ Brainyquote, Abraham Lincoln Quotes https://www.brainyquote.com/quotes/abraham_lincoln_145909
- ❖ Stonewall Jackson / Wikipedia: https://en.wikipedia.org/wiki/Stonewall_Jackson
- ❖ Top 25 Quotes By Clara Barton | A-Z Quotes http://www.azquotes.com/author/998-Clara_Barton

- Civil War Quotes: http://www.americancivilwarstory.com/civil-war-quotes.html -"fighting" Joe Hooker
- Robert E. Lee Quotes — American Civil War Stories http://www.americancivilwarstory.com/civil-war-quotes.html
- Drum Taps Quotes by Walt Whitman — Goodreads https://www.goodreads.com/quotes/tag/civil-war Walt Whitman_Drum Taps
- Top 21 Quotes by Mary Boykin Chesnut | A-Z Quotes http://www.azquotes.com/author/42457-Mary_Boykin_Chesnut

Internet Sources for
Photos & Historical Information

- Madison County Historical Society, Andersonville http://www.andersonmchs.com/andersonville-hoosiers.php
- Academy of American Poets / Captain! My Captain! By Walt Whitman — Poems https://www.poets.org/poetsorg/poem/o-captain-my-captain
- The Walt Whitman Archive https://whitmanarchive.org/multimedia/image036.html?sort=year &order=ascending&page=4
- The Wound-dresser By Walt Whitman — Poetry Foundation, https://www.poetryfoundation.org/poems/53027/the-wound-dresser
- University of Maryland Libraries, On The Front — Women And The Civil War https://www.lib.umd.edu/civilwarwomen/womens-histories/roles-on-the-front
- Sherman's March to the Sea — Wikipedia https://en.wikipedia.org/wiki/Sherman%27s_March_to_the_Sea
- Vicksburg Campaign — American Civil War — History.com, https://www.history.com/topics/american-civil-war/vicksburg-campaign
- Robert E. Lee — Civil War Trust, https://www.civilwar.org/learn/biographies/robert-e-lee
- Grant Versus Lee | Civil War Trust, https://www.civilwar.org/learn/articles/grant-versus-lee
- Louisa May Alcott — Hospital Sketches — Digital Library http://digital.library.upenn.edu/women/alcott/sketches/sketches.html
- Battle of Stones River — American Civil War — History.com http://www.history.com/topics/american-civil-war/battle-of-stones-river

- ❖ Civil War Doctors, Civil War Nurses, Nurses of The Civil War, http://www.totalgettysburg.com/civil-war-doctors.html
- ❖ Stonewall Jackson — History.net http://www.historynet.com/stonewall-jackson
- ❖ Grant and Lee Clash in the Wilderness Forest — May 05 — History https://www.history.com/this-day-in-history/grant-and-lee-clash-in-the-wilderness
- ❖ Library of Congres — Photo Archives https://www.archives.gov/research/alic/reference/photography
- ❖ Mary Virginia Wade — Civil War Wiki http://www.civilwarwiki.net/wiki/Mary_Virginia_Wade
- ❖ Richard Rowland Kirkland Wikipedia Encyclopedia https://en.wikepedia.org/wike/Richard_Rowland_Kirkland
- ❖ Richard Rowland Kirkland — Fredricksburg http://www.fredericksburg.com/civil_war/the-angel-of-marye-s-heights/article_0927a4fc-231a-5ccf-a380-562d299a6364.html
- ❖ 'Richmond At Last!': The Final, Fiery Days of The Confederacy, http://www.washingtonpost.com/sf/style/2015/03/27/wars-end/
- ❖ President Lincoln Tours Richmond — Apr 04, 1865 - History.com, https://www.history.com/this-day-in-history/president-lincoln-tours-richmond
- ❖ Maryland Historical Society — Asia Clarke Booth http://www.mdhs.org/search/node/Asia%20Booth%20Clarke%20letters-Maryland Historical Society
- ❖ Michael Dougherty Civil Prisoner http://publicdomainreview.org/collections/prison-diary-of-michael-dougherty-1908/
- ❖ Civil War Collection, Photos — Library of Congress https://www.loc.gov/collections/civil-war/about-this-collection/
- ❖ William Shakespeare – MIT / Edu http://shakespeare.mit.edu/hamlet/full.html
- ❖ Sullivan Ballou Letter — Civil War Trust www.civilwar.org/learn/primary-sources/sullivan-ballou-letter
- ❖ Remembering the Only Civilian to Die at Gettysburg — History https://www.history.com/news/remembering-the-only-civilian-to-die-at-gettysburg
- ❖ Jesse Greenspan - http://www.history.com/news/remembering-the-only-civilian-to-die-at-gettysbu
- ❖ Richard Garrett https://boothiebarn.com/tag/garretts/
- ❖ Battles — Civil War Trust www.civilwar.org/learn/civil-war/battles/shilohhttps
- ❖ The Petersen House — National Park Service www.nps.gov/foth/the-petersen-house.htm

- ❖ Wilmer Mclean — Wikipedia
  https://en.wikipedia.org/wiki/Wilmer_McLean
- ❖ Civil War Doctors — Total Gettysburg
  http://www.totalgettysburg.com/civil-war-doctors.html
- ❖ Traveling with the Wounded: Walt — Whitmanarchive.org
  http://whitmanarchive.org/criticism/current/anc.00156.html
- ❖ Civil War Medicine — Civil War Trust
  https://www.civilwar.org/learn/articles/civil-war-medicine
- ❖ Walt Whitman and President Lincoln — Lincoln Cottage
  http://www.lincolncottage.org/walt-whitman-and-president-lincoln/
- ❖ Battle of Stones River Audio — History.com
  http://www.history.com/topics/american-civil-war/battle-of-stones-river
- ❖ The Destruction of Atlanta Begins — Nov 12, 1864 — History.com
  http://www.history.com/this-day-in-history/the-destruction-of-atlanta-begins
- ❖ Battle Of Gettysburg - American Civil War - History.com
  http://www.history.com/topics/american-civil-war/battle-of-gettysburg
- ❖ Vicksburg Campaign - American Civil War - History.com
  http://www.history.com/topics/american-civil-war/vicksburg-campaign
- ❖ Battle Of Antietam — Wikipedia
  https://en.wikipedia.org/wiki/Battle_of_Antietam
- ❖ Lucy Lambert Hale — The Full Wiki
  http://www.thefullwiki.org/Lucy_Lambert_Hale
- ❖ Michael Dougherty — Bristol, Pa – Waymarking
  http://www.waymarking.com/waymarks/WM3TQ9_Michael_Dougherty_Bristol_PA
- ❖ Michael Dougherty — Wikipedia
  https://www.bristolaoh.org/michael-dougherty
- ❖ Prison Diary — Library of Congress archives
  https://archive.org/details/prisondiaryofmic00doug
- ❖ Walt Whitman http://www.waltwhitman.com/
- ❖ Joseph Hooker - Wikipedia -
  https://en.wikipedia.org/wiki/Joseph_Hooker
- ❖ Louisa May Alcott and the American Civil War - history in an Hour
  http://www.historyinanhour.com/2011/11/22/louisa-may-alcott-american-civil-war/
- ❖ The Gilder Lehrman Institute of American History / I take up my pen: Letters from the Civil War

http://oa.gilderlehrman.org/history-by-era/american-civil-war/interactives/i-take-my-pen-letters-from-civil-war

❖ Abraham Lincoln Association — Springfield, Il
http://www.abrahamlincolnassociation.org/

❖ U.S National Library of Medicine — History of Medicine
https://www.nlm.nih.gov/exhibition/lifeandlimb/maimedmen.html

❖ Clara Barton - Wikipedia
https://en.wikipedia.org/wiki/Clara_Barton

❖ Robert Hendershot, "Drummer Boy of the Rappahannock"
http://soldiers.dodlive.mil/2013/12/the-beats-of-battle-images-of-army-drummer-boys-endure/robert-hendershot-drummer-boy-of-the-rappahannock/

❖ Abraham Lincoln — Abraham Lincoln Speaks Words that Transformed a Nation — The Gilder Lehrman Institute of American History, The Morgan Library and Museum
http://abrahamlincoln.org/lincoln-speaks/lincoln-offers-words-comfort/

❖ Letters Home — New York State Library
http://www.nysl.nysed.gov/mssc/bullrun/13tent.htm

❖ Civil War Letter — Envelope — American Civil War
https://americancivilwar.com/kids_zone/soldiers_letters_civil_war.html

❖ General Robert E. Lee — Smithsonian Institution
https://www.smithsonianmag.com/smithsonian-institution/gentlemans-agreement-ended-civil-war-180954810/

❖ Garretts — Boothiebarn — Page 2,
https://boothiebarn.com/tag/garretts/page/2/

❖ Places — Ford's Theatre (U.S. National Park Service),
https://www.nps.gov/foth/learn/historyculture/places.htm

❖ The Surrenders, Part I — Huffington Post
https://www.huffingtonpost.com/entry/the-surrenders-part-i_usr55_59ef6ab4e4b00a4ce5

CPSIA information can be obtained
at www.ICGtesting.com
Printed in the USA
BVHW041934100419
545183BV00007B/115/P

9 781943 504312